SOUND

T0382192

SOUND

by

A. E. E. McKENZIE, M.A.

Trinity College, Cambridge
Assistant Master at Repton School

"The intervals in music are rather to be judged
intellectually through numbers than sensibly
through the ear"   PYTHAGORAS

CAMBRIDGE

AT THE UNIVERSITY PRESS

1936

CAMBRIDGE
UNIVERSITY PRESS

University Printing House, Cambridge CB2 8BS, United Kingdom

Cambridge University Press is part of the University of Cambridge.

It furthers the University's mission by disseminating knowledge in the pursuit of education, learning and research at the highest international levels of excellence.

www.cambridge.org
Information on this title: www.cambridge.org/9781107452480

© Cambridge University Press 1936

First published 1936
First paperback edition 2014

A catalogue record for this publication is available from the British Library

ISBN 978-1-107-45248-0 Paperback

CONTENTS

SOUND

PREFACE

This book completes my School Certificate trilogy, Heat, Light, and Sound.

The treatment throughout is simple and introductory, but by the addition of paragraphs in small type, e.g. on the Doppler effect, Kundt's dust tube, temperament, etc., I have been able to cover most of the ground (with the exception of the mathematics) likely to be needed by a boy at school—both for Higher Certificate and University Scholarships. The full account of the ear in the last chapter should be especially useful to 1st M.B. candidates.

I have used f, the internationally adopted symbol, in preference to n, to denote frequency.

As in the previous volumes I have received considerable help from Mr D. G. A. Dyson, of King Edward VI School, Stratford-on-Avon, to whom I express my thanks. He has read through the manuscript and made numerous criticisms and suggestions. The oscillograms, Figs. 72 and 74, were taken by his pupil, Mr J. W. Findlay, with apparatus made by Mr Findlay himself.

I am grateful to my colleagues, Dr A. W. Barton and Mr R. E. Williams, who have read the manuscript, and made valuable criticisms.

My pupil Mr T. H. Fisher kindly drew for me Figs. 10 and 58. These diagrams were devised as a text-book counterpart to the mechanical models often used to demonstrate wave motion.

The idea of using letters to demonstrate the growth of a transverse wave, as in Fig. 6, I obtained from Mr F. W. Westaway's book, *The Endless Quest*.

Sir William Bragg kindly lent me a photograph from which Fig. 16 was drawn, and Prof. Andrade the photograph of the dust tube for Fig. 60.

The three "sparkographs", Figs. 12, 13 and 14, were taken by the late Capt. Philip P. Quayle, and prints were lent to me, and permission given to reproduce them, by the Peters Ballistic Institute, Ohio, U.S.A.

Mr B. F. Brown, of the Science School, Repton, took the photograph of the sensitive flames in Fig. 36.

PREFACE

I am also indebted to the following publishers and firms for the loan of, and permission to reproduce, photographs and diagrams: The McGraw Hill Book Co. Inc., Messrs Longmans Green and Co., Messrs Macmillan and Co. Ltd., Messrs G. Bell and Sons, the Editor of *Flight*, the Submarine Signal Co., the Gramophone Company, the Columbia Gramophone Company, Messrs Newalls Insulation Co. Ltd., Messrs Henry Willis and Sons, Ltd., and Messrs Metropolitan Vickers Electric Co. Ltd., and the Bell Telephone Laboratories of New York.

Finally I must express my thanks to the following examining bodies for permission to reproduce School Certificate questions: The Northern University Joint Matriculation Board (N.), the University of London (L.), the Cambridge Local (C.) and Oxford Local (O.) Examination Syndicates. The letters in brackets will be found printed after the questions to designate their source.

A. E. E. M.

Repton
February 1936

SOUND

Chapter I

SOUND WAVES

Introduction.

The study of sound has assumed a sudden practical importance in the last twenty years.

During the Great War the method of locating submarines by sounds transmitted through the sea, and of detecting the position of enemy guns by the noise of their discharge, led to the application of theory and proved a great incentive to further research.

Since the War the development of the gramophone, the rise of broadcasting and talking films, the increasing menace to health of the noise of traffic and machinery, have given still greater practical importance to the study of sound.

Sound is a disturbance in the air (or some other medium).

Sound is created only when something moves—a book is dropped on the floor, a pistol is fired, or a bell quivers after being struck. Each of these movements disturbs the air, the resulting air disturbance enters the ear and agitates the ear drum, the auditory nerve is excited, and we experience the sensation of sound. It is the air disturbance, the physical cause of the sensation of sound, that we study in a book of physics: the sensation itself and its reception by the human body are studied in the sciences of psychology and physiology.

That the air (or some other medium) is indispensable for the propagation of sound may be proved by the following experiment. Place an electric bell under a glass jar (see Fig. 1) and set the bell ringing. The sound is clearly heard. Exhaust the

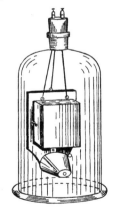

Fig. 1. The jar is placed over the receiver of an air pump and exhausted.

jar with a pump: the sound will become gradually fainter. If the bell rests on a glass or metal plate its vibrations will be communicated through the plate to the outside air, and the sound will be heard faintly even when the jar is as completely exhausted as possible. If, however, the bell is laid on a thick sheet of felt (which is almost incapable of vibration), or suspended by threads, the sound of the bell will be almost completely extinguished.

Sound can be transmitted through liquids and solids as well as gases—a phenomenon which we shall consider in the next chapter.

Sources of sound vibrate.

The prongs of a sounding tuning-fork and the plucked string of a banjo can actually be seen to vibrate. The vibrations of a drum or a bell may not be visible but they can often be felt: when they are checked by the hand the sound ceases.

A vibration is a to-and-fro motion which is continually repeated.

The motion of a fairly heavy body suspended from a spiral spring, when the body is pulled down and released (see Fig. 2), is an instructive example of vibration since it takes place slowly. The time taken by each vibration, i.e. a complete up and down motion, is known as the **period** or **periodic time**. The **number of vibrations made per sec.** is known as the **frequency**: it is denoted by **f** and is measured in cycles per sec. (c.p.s.). The extent of the vibration, i.e. the distance from the undisturbed position of the body to the upper *or* lower limit of its vibration, is called the **amplitude,** *a* (see Fig. 2).

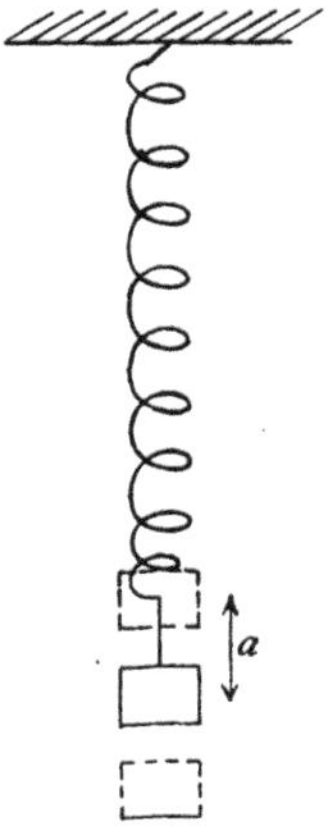

The nature of the vibrations of the prongs of a tuning-fork may be investigated by attaching to one of the prongs a bristle, and drawing under it a smoked glass plate while the prongs are vibrating (see Fig. 3). If the glass plate is moved with a uniform velocity the trace made by the bristle will be similar to that shown in Fig. 4,

Fig. 2

known to mathematicians as a sine-curve. This particular type of vibration is the simplest possible, and is called Simple Harmonic Motion.

It will be seen that the prong is moving most rapidly when passing through its normal rest position C. It moves from A to B and from B to C in equal times.

The period or time of vibration of the prongs of the fork is found to be independent of the amplitude. Thus the frequency remains constant as the vibrations become smaller. Such vibrations are said to be *isochronous*.

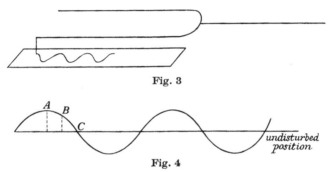

Fig. 3

Fig. 4

The nature of vibration.

In order that a body or medium may vibrate it must possess two properties: (1) inertia or mass, and (2) elasticity, i.e. power to resist change of size or shape and to recover its original condition when disturbed.

We can illustrate this fact by considering again the vibrations of a system consisting of a body suspended from the end of a spiral spring. Suppose the body is pulled down and released: the spring, owing to its elasticity, pulls the body up again. When the body reaches its original position, however, owing to the momentum acquired by its mass, it overshoots the mark and is gradually brought to rest by gravity and the resistance of the spring. Since the weight is above its position of equilibrium it again falls, overshoots this position, and stretches the spring until it is brought to rest, when the whole cycle is repeated. If the spring were non-elastic and made of lead it would not vibrate, nor would a very light spring, with no mass on the end, vibrate properly.

Air has mass and is also an elastic substance. That is why we ride on air in a motor car: under the action of a severe jolt it is

compressed and then expands again. Hence the vibrations of a
tuning-fork or some similar source can readily be communicated
to the air. The frequency of the air vibrations is equal to the
frequency of the vibrations of the source. The value of this frequency determines the pitch of the note (see p. 51).

Transverse water waves.

The passage of vibrations through the air is a form of wave
motion. It is helpful to begin the study of wave motion by
examining visible waves—those on the surface of water, for
example.

Allow a drop of water to fall into a bowl of water from a height
of about 1 ft. A train of one or two circular ripples will spread
outwards from the spot where the drop entered the water.

A small piece of paper floating on the surface of the water is

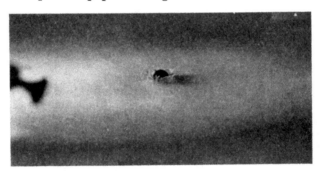

Time = 0.

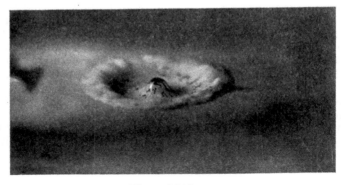

Time = 0·064 sec.

Time = 0·103 sec.

Time = 0·197 sec.

Time = 0·217 sec.

From A Study of Splashes, *A. M. Worthington, by courtesy of Messrs Longmans Green and Co.*

Fig. 5. Photographs showing how waves are set up when a drop falls into water: the wave disturbance moves over the surface while the water itself merely oscillates up and down. (The drop of water was about ½ in. in diameter and was covered with soot; note the black specks in the photographs. It fell about 16 in. into a mixture of water and milk.)

not swept outwards as the ripples pass. It merely bobs up and down. Thus, although the disturbance is moving over the surface of the water, the water does not move with it.

The phenomenon is called a **wave motion. The characteristic of all wave motions is that a disturbance travels through a medium without the medium moving bodily with it.**

The remarkable photographs in Fig. 5 taken by Professor Worthington show how the waves in the bowl originate and how they are transmitted. A small drop was allowed to fall into water, and photographs of the disturbance taken at the time of impact and at intervals of 0·064, 0·103, 0·197, 0·217 sec. after impact. Where the drop enters the water a hole is made. The water then rises up into a heap and continues to vibrate up and down for a short time, one vibration only being shown in the figure. Circular waves are seen spreading out, and these are formed by each particle of the water as it vibrates up and down, dragging its neighbour after it. Thus the appearance of the disturbance is caused by the successive vibrations of the water particles, the vibration of each particle being a little behind, or out of step with, that of the particle from which it has received its motion.

On p. 7 is shown a diagrammatic representation of the growth and travel of a wave. The letters a, b, c, etc. represent surface-water particles. Suppose a is forced downwards—as happened when the drop entered the water. It will begin to oscillate up and down, i.e. vibrate. The lines of letters show its successive positions. In the second line it has moved down: in the third line it has reached its lowest point and meanwhile the motion has been communicated to b which has also moved down. In the fourth line a has moved up, b has reached its lowest point and c has begun to move down.

It will be seen that the vibrations of the particles, each one a little out of step or *phase* with its predecessor, constitute a wave which travels along from left to right.

The best way of obtaining a grasp of wave motion is to draw these patterns for yourself on graph paper.

The distance from a to i in the last line is called the **wavelength** and is denoted by λ (see also Fig. 89). It will be seen that the wave travels forward a distance equal to the wave-length while each letter, e.g. the letter a, makes one complete vibration.

a b c d e f g h i j k l m

   b c d e f g h i j k l m
a

      c d e f g h i j k l m
   b
a

         d e f g h i j k l m
a   c
   b

a   d e f g h i j k l m
   b
      c

a
   b   f g h i j k l m
      c
         d e

a
   b
      c   g h i j k l m
         d
            e f

   b
a   c
         d   h i j k l m
            e
               f g

      c
   b   d
a   e   i j k l m
               f
                  g   h

Fig. 6. The growth and travel of a transverse wave.

Hence if each particle make f vibrations per sec. (the frequency), f waves are generated per sec. After 1 sec. f waves, each λ cm. long, will stretch from the source: the front of the first wave is then $f\lambda$ cm. from the source. The distance travelled, therefore, by the disturbance per sec., i.e. the velocity, v, is given by the equation

$$v = f\lambda.$$

Waves of this kind in which the direction of vibration of the particles is at right angles to the direction of travel of the waves are known as *transverse* waves. The wave sent down a long rope by waggling one end with the hand is a further example. It is obvious in this case that the particles of the rope do not move along with the wave.

In the case of water waves, the water particles do not vibrate strictly in straight lines, but in circles which lie in a vertical plane (see Fig. 7).

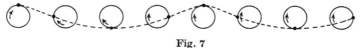

Fig. 7

Sound waves.

Sound is a form of wave motion. The photographs in Fig. 8 show a sound wave in the air spreading outwards like a water wave.

The wave consists of a single pulse of compressed air caused by the sharp crack of an electric spark (situated behind the black disc to shield its light from the camera). The wave is illuminated by another spark discharged at a very short, controlled fraction of a second after the "sound" spark, a shadow of the pulse being thereby thrown on to a photographic plate.

Sound waves are known as *longitudinal* waves, since the vibration of the air particles takes place along the direction of travel of the wave.

The nature of continuous sound waves.

The sound waves generated by a continuously vibrating body, such as a tuning-fork, consist of a succession of pulses of compressed air or compressions, separated by regions of rarefied air or rarefactions (see Fig. 9).

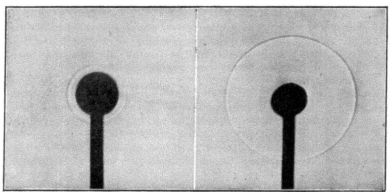

Figs. 8, 22, 27 and 34 are taken from Knowlton's Physics for College Students, *by courtesy of the McGraw Hill Book Co. Inc.*

(a)   (b)

Fig. 8. Photographs of a sound wave, caused by a spark, spreading out from a point behind the black disc. The wave takes a few thousandths of a second to pass from the position shown in (a) to that in (b).

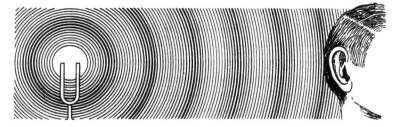

Fig. 9. Continuous sound waves, consisting of alternate compressions and rarefactions, generated by a tuning fork in air.

When the prongs move outwards they compress the air, and this compression travels outwards in a manner similar to that of the single compression sent out by the spark in Fig. 8. When the prongs move inwards the air near to them moves back again,

causing a rarefaction. All the air particles move back in turn'
with the result that the rarefaction travels outwards. Again
the prongs move outwards, and a second compression is sent
out, and so on.

The distance between the centres of two adjacent compressions
or rarefactions is called the wave-length of the sound. It is
clear that the sound wave travels a distance equal to the wave-
length while the fork makes one complete vibration.

If a fork with a higher frequency, i.e. one that vibrates more
quickly, is used, it is found that the velocity of the sound wave
is unchanged. The wave-length must therefore be less in this
case: the compressions are more numerous and closer together.
For the velocity with which the wave travels does not depend
on the rate at which the compressions are sent out from the
source but on the rate at which the motion is passed on through
the air.

Fig. 10 is a diagrammatic demonstration of the way in which
longitudinal waves are transmitted. In order to show their
speed and direction the particles of the medium are represented
by little men.

In the top line the particles are in their undisturbed position,
but we imagine that the first particle has been given a push by
a prong of a tuning-fork (shown at the side) which is moving
rapidly outwards through its position of rest.

In the second line the first particle has slowed down, and this
is due to the fact that it has been pushing the second particle
and set it moving. To make the diagram clear we have had to
separate the particles considerably, with the result that this
pushing process cannot be represented visibly. The second
particle, owing to its inertia, has not moved appreciably in the
second line but it has acquired a considerable speed.

In the third line the first particle has come to rest (for it has
ceased to be pushed by the tuning-fork), the second particle
has slowed down and the third particle has been started.

In the fourth line the first particle is seen moving back. The
prong of the tuning-fork is moving inwards, leaving an empty
space which the first particle (having bounced back off the
second particle) moves back to fill.

If the position of the first particle is noted in successive lines,
it will be seen to be vibrating backwards and forwards about

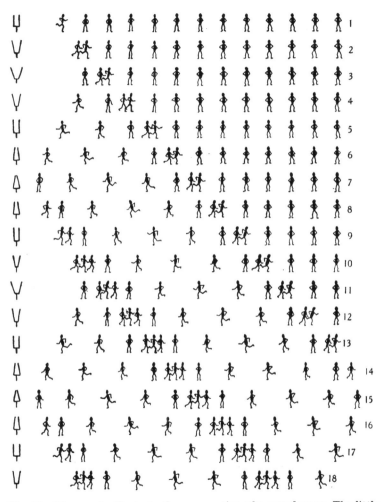

Fig. 10. Diagram to illustrate the propagation of a sound wave. The little men represent layers of air. Note the compressions and rarefactions travelling from left to right, while each man merely oscillates forwards and backwards about his mean position.

its mean position. Similarly the second, third, etc., particles are vibrating, but each one is a stage behind its predecessor.

It will be seen that this successive to-and-fro vibration of the particles gives rise to compressions and rarefactions which travel from left to right. Note how, in the rarefactions, the particles are moving back, and how the bunching-up process in the compressions takes place.

The particles in our diagrammatic arrangement represent layers of air. Each one would contain billions of molecules (the molecule being the ultimate unit of which matter is composed). For 1 cu. in. of air at ordinary atmospheric pressure contains over 440 million billion molecules, and the distance between successive compressions in a sound wave may be anything from about $\frac{1}{2}$ in. to 70 ft. according to the pitch of the sound.

The vibration of the layers of air is possible because (1) the air is elastic or compressible and after being compressed expands again, (2) the air has mass and therefore, on expanding, overshoots its undisturbed position and hence becomes rarefied.

Lord Rayleigh has estimated that the full extent of the vibration of each layer of air for sounds of ordinary loudness is only about $\frac{1}{1000}$ in. and may be as small as $\frac{1}{1,000,000}$ in. The velocity of such a layer even at its maximum must therefore be very small (of the order of $\frac{1}{1000}$ in. per sec.), compared with the velocity with which the vibration is passed on from layer to layer.

Thus the ear is a very delicate instrument: it can detect a sound with a pressure variation of only $\frac{1}{1000}$ millionth of an atmosphere. Dr Kaye has stated that if the whole population of Greater London shouted at the top of their voices the power generated would be only 1 H.P.

The displacement diagram.

It is convenient to represent a longitudinal wave by a transverse wave form, i.e. a wavy line such as that shown in Fig. 11.

Fig. 11 is a representation of the state of the longitudinal wave in the thirteenth line in Fig. 10. The numbered points represent the undisturbed positions of the particles. The actual longitudinal displacements of the little men are plotted in Fig. 11 up and down, forward displacements being plotted upward, and backward displacements downward.

Note that both the points numbered 1, 5, 9 and 13 and the corresponding little men are in their mean positions, though moving quickly. Those numbered 3, 7 and 11 are in their extreme positions, and so on. Such a graph is called a *displacement diagram*.

Note also that 5 and 13 represent the middle of compressions (because the particles on either side are displaced towards one another), and that 9 represents the middle of a rarefaction. Thus the compressions and rarefactions do not coincide with the crests and troughs, respectively, in the displacement diagram.

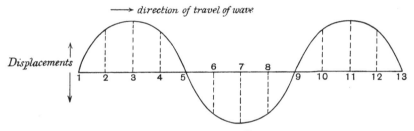

Fig. 11. Displacement diagram.

SUMMARY

Sound consists of longitudinal waves in some medium.

Each particle of the medium vibrates backwards and forwards in the direction of travel of the wave and passes on the disturbance to the adjacent particle, which vibrates a little out of phase with its neighbour. The positions of the particles at any instant may be represented by a displacement curve.

If f is the frequency of oscillation of the particles, λ the wavelength and v the velocity of the waves,

$$v = f\lambda.$$

QUESTIONS

1. What is a "vibration"?

A steel ruler is clamped at one end in a vice and set vibrating. Explain clearly what is meant by the frequency, period and amplitude of the vibrations.

2. Explain carefully the two properties a medium must possess in order to transmit waves. Would you expect sound waves to pass through (a) steel, (b) felt?

3. Explain carefully:

(a) The time at which an explosion occurs can often be ascertained by looking at the trace of a barograph—i.e. a self-recording barometer.

(b) A bee in flight sets up a humming sound: a mosquito in flight also generates a note but of higher pitch.

4. Explain what you understand by wave motion, using as an example the ripples formed when a stone is dropped into water. How do the sound waves from a tuning-fork differ from these?

Define frequency, wave-length and wave-velocity, stating the relation between them.   (L.)

5. A stone is thrown into a lake and after 4 sec. 40 ripples have spread out from the place where the stone entered the water. The radius of the outermost ripple is 1·6 metres. Find velocity and wave-length of the ripples. Find also the frequency and period of oscillation of the water particles.

6. Explain how sound is transmitted through the air from a vibrating body to the ear. Where possible, illustrate by a brief reference to experiments which support your description.   (L.)

7. Taking the velocity of sound as 1120 ft. per sec., find the wave-length of the following sounds:

(a) A man's normal voice, frequency 140 c.p.s.

(b) The highest musical note used on a piccolo, frequency 4750 c.p.s.

(c) The lowest note of a piano, frequency 27 c.p.s.

8. How do sound waves and light waves differ in respect of (a) type of waves, (b) medium, (c) speed, (d) wave-length, (e) frequency?

9. Draw the displacement diagram representing the positions of the little men in the tenth line of Fig. 10.

Chapter 11

SOUND VELOCITY AND SIGNALLING

Sound, like every other form of wave motion, takes time to travel from one place to another. Its speed—about 750 m.p.h. or $\frac{1}{5}$ mile per sec.—is very pedestrian, however, compared with that of light and wireless waves. The latter travel at 186,000 miles per sec. Thus in 5 sec. sound travels about 1 mile and light about 1,000,000 miles.

Determination of the velocity of sound in air.

In the year 1708 Derham determined the velocity of sound by observing the time interval between seeing the flash and hearing the report of a distant cannon. He made his observations from the top of the tower of Upminster Church in Essex, and the cannon was fired on Blackheath, distant some $12\frac{1}{2}$ miles across the Thames.

The time taken by light to travel $12\frac{1}{2}$ miles is about $\frac{1}{15,000}$ sec., and is therefore negligible. The observed time interval was therefore the time taken by the sound. This interval varied between $55\frac{1}{2}$ and 63 sec. according to the direction of the wind. Derham obtained as his average value of the velocity of sound 1142 ft. per sec.

The effect of the wind may be eliminated by the method of reciprocal firing, first used by a commission of the French Academy in 1738. Two cannon were used, about 17 or 18 miles apart, the velocity of sound in opposite directions determined, and the average of the two results calculated.

The chief source of error in these cannon experiments is the "personal equation" of the observers. Suppose an observer is using a stop-watch. He takes a short but definite interval of time after seeing the flash to start his watch, and in all probability a different interval of time to stop his watch on hearing the report. These errors, which vary with different observers, and also, it has been found, with the loudness of the sound, are called the "personal equation".

Regnault, in the middle of the nineteenth century, made several determinations of the velocity of sound both in the open air, and in the new, empty water pipes of Paris. He attempted to eliminate the personal equation by using a rubber membrane instead of an observer. When the sound wave struck the membrane the latter moved, broke an electric circuit, and hence caused a mark to be made on a revolving drum. The time of the report was also recorded on the drum by stretching a wire forming part of an electric circuit over the muzzle of the gun in such a way that it was broken when the gun was fired. But the membrane also was found to have a personal equation, and Regnault performed a number of experiments to determine it.

The methods used for the accurate determination of the velocity of sound during and after the Great War were the same in principle as that of Regnault and his predecessors, but the sound detector used was the Tucker hot-wire microphone, and the instants of the report and the arrival of the sound at the microphone were recorded on a moving strip of sensitised paper or film. We shall describe this process in detail in connection with sound ranging. In 1921 Angerer and Ladenburg obtained the value $330 \cdot 8 \pm 0 \cdot 1$ metres per sec. in dry air at $0°$ C.

The echo method.

The following is a method of determining the velocity of sound which can be performed quite simply by the reader.

If you stand 100 yards from a wall and clap your hands sharply you will hear an echo about $\frac{1}{2}$ sec. later. If you clap your hands every $\frac{1}{2}$ sec., or better, have a metronome beating $\frac{1}{2}$ secs., you can adjust your distance from the wall so that the echo of one clap is heard simultaneously with the next clap. The sound has then travelled twice the distance between you and the wall in the interval between the claps, and hence its velocity can be calculated.

The method has been refined by the use of an electro-magnetic tapper and it is claimed that timing is possible to $\frac{1}{400}$ sec.

Theoretical investigation.

Interest was first aroused in the speed at which sound travels by Sir Isaac Newton's calculation, published in his book the *Principia* in 1686, of the theoretical speed at which it might be expected to travel, assuming it to consist of compressional waves in air. This theoretical investigation showed a remarkable insight into the mechanism of wave motion, but there was a flaw in the argument. The formula

$$v = \sqrt{\frac{p}{d}},$$

where $\qquad$ $v =$ velocity of sound in air,
$p =$ pressure of the air,
$d =$ density of the air,

gave a result for the velocity which was 15 per cent. too low.

Newton made several ingenious suggestions as to the cause of the discrepancy, but it was not until 130 years later that Laplace hit upon the true cause. Newton had ignored the changes of temperature of the air caused by its very rapid compression and expansion while a sound wave passed through it. The correct formula is $v = \sqrt{\frac{\gamma p}{d}}$, where γ is a constant.

We cannot enter into the derivation of the formula, but mention it because it acted as a keen stimulus to accurate experimental determinations, and also because the fact that it gives values which agree closely with those obtained by experiment confirms the views described in the previous chapter, that sound consists of compressional waves.

It is apparent from the formula that the velocity of sound in hydrogen will be greater than in air (at the same pressure), since the density, d, of hydrogen is less than that of air. Similarly the velocities in carbon dioxide or coal gas, which are denser than air, are less than in air.

Effect of pressure, temperature and humidity on the velocity.

The velocity of sound in air does not alter when the barometric pressure changes. For a change in the pressure, p, produces a change in the density, d, in exactly the same ratio (Boyle's Law). Hence, in the formula $v = \sqrt{\frac{\gamma p}{d}}$, although p changes, $\frac{p}{d}$ remains constant. Experiments confirming that the velocity is independent of the pressure have been carried out at high altitudes (where the pressure is considerably less than at sea-level) in the Tyrol.

The velocity of sound increases, however, when the temperature of the air rises—at the rate of about 1 ft. per sec. for a rise of 1°C. This is due to the decrease in density of air when heated (the pressure remaining constant).

Suppose v_0, v_t, d_0 and d_t represent the velocities of sound and the densities of the air at $0°$ and t °C. respectively.

$$v_0 = \sqrt{\frac{\gamma p}{d_0}} \quad \text{and} \quad v_t = \sqrt{\frac{\gamma p}{d_t}}.$$

Dividing,
$$\frac{v_t}{v_0} = \sqrt{\frac{d_0}{d_t}}.$$

But
$$\frac{d_0}{d_t} = \frac{T}{273} \quad \text{(see the author's } Heat\text{),}$$

Fig. 12. Photograph of the sound wave from a revolver which has just been fired.

where $T°$ and $273°$ are the absolute temperatures corresponding to $t°$ and $0°$ C.

$$\therefore \frac{v_t}{v_0} = \sqrt{\frac{T}{273}}.$$

Thus *the velocity of sound is proportional to the square root of the absolute temperature*. Knowing the velocity of sound at $t°$ C., it is possible, by means of the above formula, to calculate the velocity of sound at $0°$ C., and *vice versa*. Experiments at low temperatures were carried out in the Arctic during Parr's voyage.

The velocity of sound also depends on the dampness of the air. The density of damp air is less than that of dry air owing to the fact that the density of water vapour is less than that of air. Hence the velocity of sound is greater in damp air than in dry air.

Sound ranging.

During the Great War the sound made by enemy guns was used to detect their position. The method is known as sound ranging, and necessitates an accurate knowledge of the velocity of sound in air.

Most modern bullets and shells travel faster than sound. They therefore give rise to V-shaped compression waves, one at the front and one at the back rather like the wake of a ship (see Fig. 13). Such a wave, known as the "onde de choc", gives rise to a noise like a loud crack.

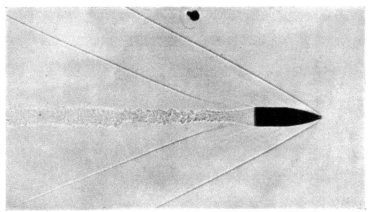

By courtesy of the Peters Ballistic Institute, Ohio

Fig. 13. Photograph of the V-shaped compression waves caused by a bullet travelling faster than sound—known as the "onde de choc". The gun wave, or "onde de bouche" (not shown in the photograph), is following on behind.

Following behind the "onde de choc" is the wave set up by the explosion at the gun. This travels at the velocity of sound, and is called the "onde de bouche" or gun wave. It is often scarcely audible and of low pitch. This wave is the one used for sound-ranging purposes.

There is also a third set of waves caused by the bursting of the shell.

It is clear that a very selective microphone (or sound detector) is required in order to distinguish the "onde de bouche" from the "onde de choc" and the shell explosion. The one used by the British armies was the Tucker hot-wire microphone. This consists of a metal box of about 16 litres capacity with a small opening

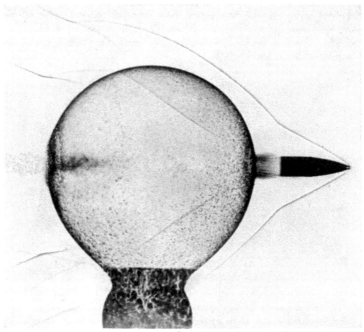

Fig. 14. The bullet has just passed through a soap bubble filled with a mixture of hydrogen and air. The speed of sound in hydrogen is greater than its speed in air and also than that of the bullet: hence the shape of the compression waves is modified as shown in the photograph.

or neck. Across the opening is stretched a small grid of fine platinum wire which is heated by an electric current. The box acts as a resonator (see p. 79), and by adjusting its volume the microphone may be made to respond only to sounds of certain pitch. When the "onde de bouche" reaches the hot platinum grid, the latter is cooled by the compression wave and its electrical resistance is thereby decreased. This causes an electric current to pass through a delicate detecting instrument known as an Einthoven galvanometer.

At least three microphones, situated on a carefully measured base line, are necessary. Suppose M_0, M_1, M_2 are the three microphones, and G is the (unknown) position of the gun (see

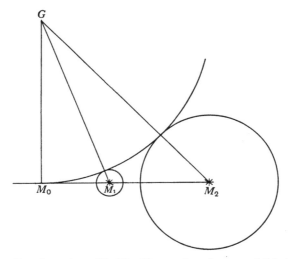

Fig. 15. Sound ranging. M_0, M_1, M_2 are microphones and G is the gun whose position is required.

Fig. 15). Suppose the sound reaches M_0 first, and that it reaches M_1 and M_2, t_1 and t_2 sec. respectively after M_0. Let the velocity of sound in air be v. With centres M_1 and M_2 draw circles of radii vt_1 and vt_2 respectively. The gun will lie at the centre of a circle touching these two circles and passing through M_0.

In practice six microphones were used, for increased certainty, on a base line about 9000 yards long, 2 or 3 miles behind the front line. They were connected by wires to the six strings of a special Einthoven galvanometer, situated in a dug-out about 1 mile further back from the front line.

The Einthoven galvanometer consists of six strings (each connected to one of the microphones), stretched at right angles to a strong magnetic field. When a current passes through one of the strings the latter is displaced and vibrates. Shadows of the strings are thrown through a fine slit by a lamp and system of lenses on to a moving photographic film. A typical record on a strip of film is shown in Fig. 16. The kinks in the dark horizontal lines record the arrivals of the sound at the six microphones. The dark vertical lines are timing lines and occur at intervals of $\frac{1}{100}$ sec. They are caused by the illumination of the lamp being cut off every $\frac{1}{100}$ sec. by the teeth of a revolving wheel whose speed is controlled by a tuning-fork.

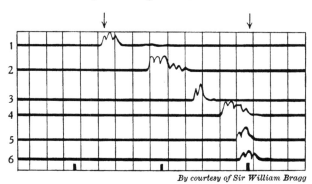

By courtesy of Sir William Bragg

Fig. 16. Sound ranging record showing the times of arrival, at six microphones, of the onde de bouche, or gun wave, from a 15 cm. howitzer.

The whole apparatus was "switched on" by an advanced observer or "sentry microphone" as soon as he heard the report of an enemy gun. Towards the end of the War the apparatus had been so perfected that the film was automatically developed and fixed, enabling the location of the enemy gun to be worked out in a few minutes.

The value of the velocity of sound used in the calculations had to be corrected for the temperature and humidity of the air, and the direction and velocity of the wind. Nevertheless, guns situated from 3 to 10 miles from the microphones could be located to within about 100 yards.

The Cumbrae talking beacon.

Sound ranging has been put to good use in peace, as well as in war. Indeed, it is to be hoped that its employment in war will never again be necessary.

At the Cumbrae lighthouse on the Clyde there is a talking beacon which speaks the word "Cumbrae" through a fog-horn and, simultaneously, broadcasts it by wireless.

These two messages may be picked up by ships in the vicinity and the time interval between them is the time taken by sound to travel from the lighthouse to the ship. Hence, knowing the velocity of sound, the navigators of the ship can determine their distance from the lighthouse. The beacon is meant for use in fog.

The binaural effect.

We are able to detect the direction from which a sound is coming because we possess two ears. The sound enters one ear a fraction of a second before it enters the other. If we are standing at right angles to the direction of the sound, however, it is impossible to tell whether the sound is coming from in front of or behind us, since it enters both ears simultaneously.

The effect is used to detect the position of invisible aeroplanes. Two pairs of collecting trumpets (see Fig. 17) act as two pairs of large ears situated several feet apart and hence exaggerate the binaural effect. Each pair of trumpets is connected by tubes to the ears of two observers. One observer can swivel all the trumpets sideways and the other observer tilts them up and down. As the observers adjust the position of the trumpets the sound will be heard more strongly first in one ear and then in the other. In the position of balance, when the sound is heard equally in both ears, the axes of the trumpets will be pointing towards the aeroplane. Since however an aeroplane travels swiftly and sound takes an appreciable time to reach the detector, the aeroplane will always be slightly in advance of the position found.

Determination of the velocity of sound in water.

The velocity of sound in water is more than four times its velocity in air—about 4700 ft. per sec. This is due to the fact that water, although denser than air, has a much greater elasticity.

The first accurate determinations were carried out in 1826 by Colladon and Sturm in Lake Geneva. Two boats were moored at a distance apart of about 9 miles. At one boat a bell under the water was struck and simultaneously some gunpowder was ignited (see Fig. 18 (a) and (b)). The experiments were carried out at night so that the observer on the other boat could see the flash

By courtesy of the Editor of Flight

Fig. 17. An aeroplane detector: it utilises the binaural effect.

clearly. He detected the arrival of the sound by means of a large ear-trumpet closed by a membrane and immersed in the lake. The time interval between the arrival of the flash and sound was measured by a stop-watch. It was about 9 sec. (After about half a minute more the clang of the bell was again heard faintly. Why?) The velocity of the sound was obtained by dividing the

Fig. 18 (*a*). Colladon and Sturm's experiment. When the lever was pushed down the bell was struck, and simultaneously a light was applied to the gunpowder.

From Guillemin's The Forces of Nature, *by courtesy of Messrs Macmillan and Co. Ltd.*

Fig. 18 (*b*). This observer noted the time (with the aid of the small lantern) on seeing the flash and also on hearing the sound which had travelled through the water.

distance between the boats by the time interval recorded by the stop-watch.

As a result of the development of submarine signalling by sound waves several other determinations of the velocity of sound in water have been made in recent years, notably those of Wood, Browne and Cochrane for the British Admiralty in the years 1920–2.

A depth charge was exploded from a destroyer, which simultaneously sent out a wireless signal. (Wireless waves travel at the same speed as light.) The sound was picked up by four hydrophones mounted on tripods on the sea bed, the nearest being about 12 miles from the destroyer, and the other three in the same straight line at intervals of 4 miles. The hydrophones were connected by cables to the strings of an Einthoven galvanometer (see p. 22) in the recording station at St Margaret's Bay, near Dover. The arrival of the wireless signal and the sound waves at the hydrophones caused electric currents to flow through the strings of the galvanometer, and these were recorded on a moving sensitised strip of paper, similar to that described in the account of sound ranging. Thus the times of arrival of the wireless and sound waves were known (by estimation) to $\frac{1}{1000}$ sec.

The velocity of the sound could be calculated in two ways: (1) by measuring the interval between the arrival of the wireless flash, and the arrival of the sound at any of the four microphones, (2) by measuring the interval between the arrival of the sound at any two microphones (situated 4 miles apart in a straight line with the destroyer). The latter method was considered the more accurate, since there was uncertainty as to the exact position of the charge and the exact time of firing.

Extensive measurements of the temperature and salinity of the sea, and the movement of the tides during the experiments (since all these affect the velocity), were necessary for the results to be of value.

Under-water signalling.

The sea is an excellent medium for the transmission of sound. Its temperature is comparatively uniform, and under-water currents are not so prevalent or disturbing as winds. Sounds travel much farther in water than in air, the absorption of sound in water being 2000 times less than in air.

Thus the transmission of under-water sounds has proved of value in navigation and in the detection of enemy submarines in war.

The simplest device for detecting sounds in water is a trumpet closed by a membrane similar to that used by Colladon and Sturm, in which the vibrations in the water are communicated

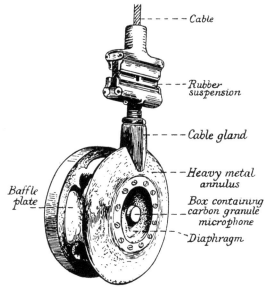

From Sound, *by A. B. Wood, by courtesy of Messrs G. Bell and Sons Ltd.*

Fig. 19. A hydrophone.

through a membrane to the air in the trumpet. The instrument which is now used, however, is *the hydrophone,* in which the vibrations in the water are transformed into electric currents.

The hydrophone consists of a rustless steel diaphragm to which is attached a watertight box containing a carbon granule microphone, the whole being held in a heavy metal annulus (see Fig. 19). When the sound vibrations in the water strike the diaphragm it vibrates and the carbon in the microphone is shaken up, thereby changing its electrical resistance. This is exactly like an ordinary telephone. The microphone is connected by wires to a battery, transformer and telephones, and the change of electrical resistance of the microphone causes a current to flow through the telephones which then give out a sound.

Fig. 19 shows a uni-directional hydrophone. A heavy baffle plate is situated behind the diaphragm, so that the latter is only affected by sounds coming from the front. Again, if the hydrophone is turned so that the diaphragm is edgewise to the on-coming sounds, it does not vibrate. It vibrates most strongly when held at right angles to the direction of the sound. Hence, by turning the hydrophone until the sounds in the telephones are loudest, the direction of the sound is known.

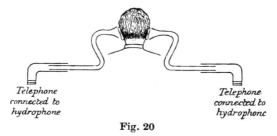

Telephone
connected to
hydrophone

Telephone
connected to
hydrophone

Fig. 20

Another method of determining the direction of under-water sounds, in particular for detecting submarines, has been developed by the American navy. The binaural effect already described (see p. 23) is utilised and two hydrophones are necessary.

The hydrophones might be suspended from the ends of a long bar which could be rotated, just as the trumpet collectors of an aeroplane detector are rotated. There is a more convenient method, however, which enables the hydrophones to be fixed to the hull of the ship.

Let us suppose that the sound reaches one microphone before the other. The sound will be heard in one telephone before the other. If, however, the telephones are connected to the ear by tubes of variable length containing air, it is possible to adjust the lengths of the tubes so that the two sounds are heard simultaneously (see Fig. 20). Knowing the ratio of the velocities of sound in air and water and the distance apart of the hydrophones, it is possible to calculate the direction of the sound.

In practice the variable air-path takes the form of a dial compensator, for use with which special tables are compiled.

The sounds made by a submarine are caused chiefly by its screw. When rotating rapidly the screw makes holes in the water, called cavitations, and powerful sounds are made by the impact of the water filling up these holes. The sounds are much reduced when the ship slackens speed. It is then very difficult to detect the submarine. For the sounds made by the searching vessel—the swish of the water against the hull, the noise of the engines and propellers—are very much louder than the sounds from the distant submarine.

Hydrophones are attached sometimes to the outside of the hull of a vessel, and sometimes just inside the hull in a tank of water. A detector in air just inside the hull is not used because there is a considerable loss of energy when sound passes from water to air. Drifters, during the Great War, carried portable hydrophones which could be lowered into the sea when required.

Echo sounding.

The old method of finding the depth of water beneath a ship was that of "heaving the lead". A heavy sinker was let down to the sea bed. In deep water a Kelvin deep-sea sounder was let down, also on a weighted line, and the operation might take several hours. By finding the time taken for a sound wave, sent by a tapper near the bottom of the ship's hull, to be reflected back from the sea bed, a determination of depth can be made in a few seconds. Moreover the ship need not reduce speed to below 15–20 knots.

The main difficulty is the measurement of the very short time interval taken by the sound. Since the velocity of sound in water is about 5000 ft. per sec., an error of $\frac{1}{100}$ sec. means an error of 25 ft. in the depth (the sound travels down and up again).

Fig. 21 illustrates the operation of the Fathometer, by means of which the depth of water beneath a ship can be found almost instantaneously. The officer on the ship's bridge closes a switch, thereby causing electric currents to flow which set the oscillator working and, simultaneously, cause a neon lamp to start rotating at a certain speed round a dial marked in fathoms (see inset in

Fig. 21. Echo sounding by means of a Fathometer.

the picture). The oscillator sends out sounds which, after reflection from the sea bed, are picked up by the hydrophone. The hydrophone thereupon operates an amplifier which causes the neon lamp to flash. The neon lamp has, by this time, travelled part of the way round the dial, and, acting like a luminous pointer, it indicates the depth.

Most great liners are now equipped with this device.

The echo sounder is also coming into use in salvage operations. The wreck of the *Lusitania*, sunk by a German submarine off the south-west coast of Ireland during the Great War, was located in October 1935 by this method. She was lying in 300 ft. of water and so great was the accuracy of the sounder that, as the salvage ship drifted over her, the outline of the wreck could be traced out.

The velocity of sound in solids.

Sound travels much more rapidly in solids than it does in gases or liquids. In iron, for example, its velocity is 5000 metres per sec., about fifteen times as great as its velocity in air.

Biot made observations of the velocity of sound in iron pipes, 3120 ft. long. One end of the pipe was struck with a hammer. At the other end, an ear placed against the pipes heard two sounds, the one which had travelled through the iron and the other which had travelled through the air. Knowing the velocity of sound in air it was possible to determine, from the time interval between the two sounds, the velocity of sound in the iron.

You should with the aid of a friend repeat the experiment on a line of iron railings.

SUMMARY

The velocity of sound in air has been determined by (1) cannon, (2) echo methods. Its value in dry air at 15° C. is 339·7 metres per sec. or 1114 ft. per sec.

The velocity of sound in air (1) is independent of the pressure, (2) is proportional to the square root of the absolute temperature, $\dfrac{V_t}{V_0} = \sqrt{\dfrac{T}{273}}$, (3) increases when the air becomes more damp.

The velocity of sound in water has been determined, using as sound detector (1) a membrane (Colladon and Sturm), (2) hydrophones (Wood, Browne and Cochrane).

Sound ranging and echo depth sounding require an accurate knowledge of the velocities of sound in air and water respectively.

The fact that sound enters one ear slightly before the other ear enables the direction of a sound to be estimated, and is known as the binaural effect.

QUESTIONS

Take the velocity of sound in air as 1100 ft. per sec. unless otherwise stated.

1. The timekeeper of a 100 yards race stands by the tape and presses his stop-watch on hearing the report of the starting pistol, instead of on seeing the flash. What error in the time of the race does this introduce?

2. The distance in miles of a lightning flash from an observer may be found approximately by counting the number of human pulse beats between the lightning flash and the thunderclap and dividing the number by 6. Justify this rule, assuming that the human pulse beats 75 times per min. and that the velocity of sound is 1080 ft. per sec.   (C.)

3. Explain carefully:

(a) A concert broadcast by wireless is heard by a listener near to his loudspeaker a fraction of a second before people at the back of the concert hall.

(b) When a long line of iron railings is tapped, two taps are heard by an ear held near to the railing some distance away.

4. Explain why the soldiers at the rear of a long column marching to the sound of a band in the front, appear out of step with those in the front.

If they are taking 120 steps per min., how far from the front will those men be who are marching in time but exactly out of step with the bandsmen?

5. How many vibrations must a fork of frequency 256 c.p.s. make before it is heard 100 ft. away?

6. A boy standing in a disused quarry claps his hands sharply once every second and hears an echo from the face of the opposite cutting. He moves until the echo is heard midway between the claps. How far is he then from the reflecting surface? (L.)

7. Explain how echoes are formed. Determine the interval between successive echoes formed by two cliffs, 1500 ft. apart, if the observer who makes the initial sound stands 500 ft. from one of them. (L.)

8. A man standing between two parallel cliffs fires a rifle. He hears one echo after $1\frac{1}{2}$ sec., one after $2\frac{1}{2}$ sec. and one after 4 sec. Explain how these echoes reach him and calculate the distance apart of the two cliffs.
The velocity of sound under the given conditions is 1120 ft. per sec. (L.)

9. In order to determine her proximity to an iceberg towards which she is heading with uniform velocity a steamer sounds her siren *once every minute*. The echo of the first blast is heard after 12 sec. and that of the second after 9 sec. Calculate the original distance of the steamer from the iceberg and also her velocity.

10. The pilot of an aeroplane, travelling horizontally at 120 m.p.h., fires a gun and hears the echo from the ground after an interval of 3 sec. Find the height of the aeroplane.

11. Explain as fully as you can the effect of the following factors on the velocity of sound in air: (a) temperature, (b) the barometric pressure, (c) fog, (d) wind.

12. Explain briefly the principle of echo sounding.
The interval between a tap made on a ship's side and the echo from the sea bed is $\frac{3}{4}$ sec. Taking the velocity of sound in water as 4700 ft. per sec., find the depth of the sea.

13. Three microphones, A, B, C, are situated at intervals of 3000 ft. in a straight line. The sound caused by the firing of a distant gun reaches B and C 0·60 sec. and 2·34 sec. after A, respectively. Show (by drawing) that the distance of the gun from A is about 5000 ft.

14. How does the velocity of sound in air vary with the temperature?
Given the velocity of sound is 342·7 metres per sec. at 20° C., calculate its velocity at 0° C.

15. An observer sets his watch by the sound of a gun fired at a fort 1 mile distant. If the temperature of the air at the time is 15° C.,

what will be the error? Mention other causes which are likely to lead to errors in the setting. (Velocity of sound in air at 0° C. = 1090 ft. per sec.) (L.)

16. Calculate the wave-lengths in air and water of sounds of frequency 20 and 20,000 c.p.s. (the highest and lowest notes audible to an average ear). Take the velocity of sound in water as 4700 ft. per sec.

17. A gun is fired near the end of a cast-iron tube 2 kilometres long, and two sounds are heard at the other end with an interval of 5·5 sec. between them. If the velocity of sound in air is 340 metres per sec., find its velocity in cast iron.

18. If the velocity of sound in air is 340 metres per sec. find its velocity in hydrogen at the same temperature.

(Density of air = 14·4 × density of hydrogen.)

Chapter III

REFLECTION, REFRACTION AND INTERFERENCE

Reflection.

On striking a surface, such as a wall, sound waves are reflected.

Fig. 22 is a photograph of the reflection of a spherical sound wave, taken by the spark method described on p. 8. The reflected wave appears to be spreading out from an "image" of

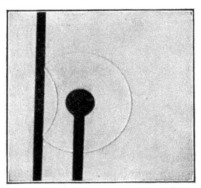

Fig. 22. The reflection of a sound wave at a plane surface.

the source of sound which is situated as far behind the reflecting surface as the source is in front. Thus the reflection of sound obeys the same laws as the reflection of light.

Echoes.

Sound heard by reflection is called an echo. The roll of thunder consists of echoes from clouds and hills of the clap set up at the flash.

A remarkable echo is that of the Whispering Gallery in the dome of St Paul's Cathedral. A whisper near the wall can be heard everywhere round the circumference of the gallery. This is due to the fact that many of the reflected rays keep near to the wall as shown in Fig. 23.

Sometimes in walking past iron railings a ringing musical sound is heard accompanying each sharp footfall. The sound wave set up when the foot strikes the pavement is reflected in turn at each bar of the railings. The reflected waves reach the ear in rapid succession and give rise to a musical note whose pitch is equal to the number arriving per sec. The phenomenon is known as the *echelon echo*.

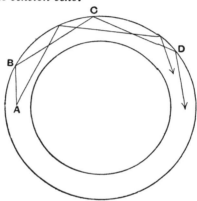

Fig. 23

Acoustics of buildings.

In an ordinary room sound undergoes 200–300 reflections before dying away. This results in a considerable prolongation of the sound known as reverberation, and a rapid uniform distribution of the sound throughout the room. Every public speaker knows that it is far less exhausting to address an audience in a hall than in the open air, because in the former one's voice is "supported" by these reflections from the walls and ceiling.

Experiments with people suspended in open space below balloons have shown that the normal voice, when it is not reinforced by reflection, is inaudible at a distance of about 11 metres. Sounds cannot be heard very far over freshly fallen snow which is a bad reflector: on the other hand, at night over smooth water sounds can be heard at a great distance.

The sound in a room becomes finally extinct, because at each reflection a fraction of the sound energy is absorbed.

A certain amount of this reverberation is desirable, especially for giving richness to music, but too much reverberation is most undesirable. If, for example, each syllable is loudly prolonged while a speaker utters the next few syllables, his speech will be confused and unintelligible. Domes and curved walls are apt to focus sounds and produce loud delayed echoes, especially at particular points.

As a result of the work of Sabine and others an important branch of sound dealing with the acoustics of buildings has been developed. This has proved of special value in the design of broadcasting and talkie studios, cinemas and theatres.

Sabine began his investigations in an attempt to remedy the defective acoustical properties of a lecture room at Harvard University. He blew an organ pipe of definite pitch and loudness in the room, and found the time which elapsed, after stopping the organ pipe, before the sound became inaudible. He called this the *time of reverberation.* For the lecture room in question the value was 5·45–5·62 sec., during which time even a slow and deliberate speaker will utter a dozen syllables.

The next problem was to reduce the time of reverberation. Sabine did this by means of cushions which absorb sound readily. He found that the time of reverberation was almost independent of the position of the source of the sound and the observer and that the effect of the cushions was almost independent of their position.

In order to put his investigations on a scientific basis Sabine had to choose a more suitable unit of absorbing power than a cushion. He chose the perfect absorber which reflects no sound at all—an open window. Each member of an audience is equivalent to $4\frac{1}{2}$ sq. ft. of open window, in respect of absorbing power, women being rather better absorbers than men on account of the nature of their dress.

If a represents the fraction of sound energy absorbed by a surface:

For an open window $a = 1$.
For thick carpets, audiences, felt, etc. $a = 0.5$.
For hard surfaces like wood, glass, metal $a = 0.01$.

In order to increase their absorbing power, when necessary, the walls and ceilings of studios, cinemas and offices in which there are many typewriters, are covered with sound-absorbing wool, asbestos felt, or asbestos spray.

In order that the reverberation times of a theatre, cinema, or up-to-date lecture room may not differ widely when empty and full, the seats are backed with plush, giving them an absorbing power equal to that of a member of the audience.

The best reverberation time of a hall depends on its function—whether it is to be used for speech or music, and also on its

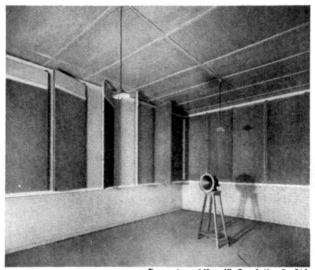

By courtesy of Newall's Insulation Co. Ltd.

Fig. 24. A variable reverberation room. The reversible panels have a very hard reflecting surface on one side and a highly absorbent surface on the other. In this room new absorbent surfaces can be tested. A loudspeaker for making sounds can be seen in the picture.

volume. The following table gives the reverberation times of several of the studios at Broadcasting House:

Studio	Principal use	Reverbera- tion time (sec.)	Volume cu. ft.
B *a*	Vaudeville. Light music	1·1	30,000
B *b*	Dance bands, octets, etc.	0·85	10,000
Concert hall	Orchestral and band performances	1·75	125,000
4*a*, 4*b*	News	Dead	670
6*c*, 7*c*	Speech in plays	Dead	1,500
8*a*	Debates and discussions	0·45	2,100

Fig. 25. The ripple tank at the National Physical Laboratory being used to test the acoustic properties of a hall, a sectional model of which may be seen in the photograph.

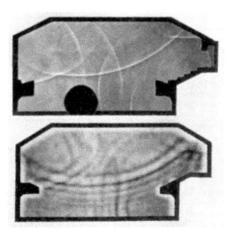

Figs. 25 and 26 are taken from The Acoustics of Buildings *by Davis and Kaye, by courtesy of Messrs G. Bell and Sons*

Fig. 26. Testing the acoustic properties of a hall. The waves in the upper photograph are reflections of a single circular wave which was sent out from a spark behind the black disc—as in Fig. 8. The lower photograph shows a test of a similar model using the ripple tank of Fig. 25.

It is possible to study by means of models the acoustic properties of a room before it is built, using either a water ripple
tank or the method of spark photography (see Figs. 25 and 26).
In this way, the track of the sound waves, their successive reflections etc. can be followed and defects in design eliminated.

The refraction of sound.

Sound, like light, is refracted on passing from one medium to
another of different density, i.e. it changes its direction at the
surface of separation of the media owing to its change of velocity
(see the author's *Light*).

Fig. 27. Refraction of a sound wave (originating behind the black disc),
on passing through a lens-shaped bag containing sulphur dioxide gas.

Fig. 27 is a photograph showing the refraction of a sound
wave on passing through a lens-shaped bag containing sulphur
dioxide, a gas which is denser than air. That part of the wave
which has passed through the lens has become flattened owing
to the fact that sound travels more slowly in sulphur dioxide
than in air. The source of the sound, a spark, is situated behind
the black disc. Note the original wave in the right-hand top and
bottom corners of the picture. Note also the reflected wave, of
different curvature from the original wave, to the right of the
black disc. The reflection took place at the front surface of the
lens which acted as a convex mirror. There is another interesting

feature of this photograph, the little clefts and increased curvature of the original wave where it joins the refracted wave. This is due to the change of direction and spreading of the original wave at the edge of the lens, a phenomenon known as diffraction. Diffraction occurs in the case of light but on a much smaller scale, since the wave-length of light is much shorter than that of sound.

If we borrow a conception used in the study of light and consider rays of sound at right angles to the wave fronts, we can represent the photograph by the diagram of Fig. 28. Since the refracted wave front in the photograph is very nearly plane, the refracted rays are nearly parallel to the axis of the lens and the spark must therefore be situated near the principal focus of the lens.

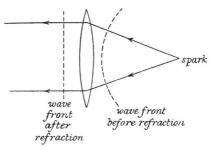

Fig. 28

Sound does not readily pass from one medium to another if its velocities in the two media are markedly different. Thus when a sound wave in the air strikes the surface of water most of the sound energy is reflected and very little is refracted into the water. To a swimmer under the water the sound would probably be inaudible. Similarly, sound does not pass readily from water to air. This fact is of importance in the design of under-water sound receivers, such as hydrophones.

Refraction in the atmosphere.

(*a*) *Temperature gradient.* Sound travels more rapidly in warm air than in cold, and hence refraction takes place in the atmosphere, wherever it is not at a uniform temperature.

In Fig. 29 (a) sound waves are shown passing from a layer of warm air to a layer of cold air. The end of each wave front which reaches the cold air first is retarded since it travels more slowly

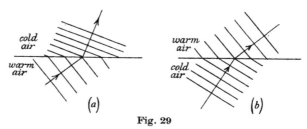

Fig. 29

in cold air than in warm. Hence the wave front is slewed round and the direction of travel of the sound wave changes as shown in the figure. Similarly, when a wave front passes from cold air

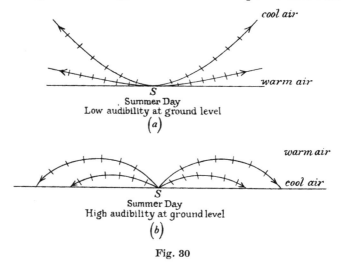

Fig. 30

to warm air (see Fig. 29 (b)), the end which reaches the warm air first gains on the rest of the wave front and the whole front wheels as shown.

On a summer day the ground becomes hot and heats the air

near to it. There is consequently a temperature gradient in the atmosphere, the air becoming cooler as we rise. At night the ground cools rapidly and the temperature gradient is reversed. Why? (see the author's *Heat*).

Thus on a summer day waves emitted by a source, *S*, near the ground (see Fig. 30 (*a*)), wheel upwards. Conditions are similar to those in Fig. 29 (*a*), but since the change of temperature in the atmosphere is gradual, the sound in Fig. 30 (*a*) is bent gradually and follows a curved path.

On a summer evening, since the air near the ground is cooler than the air above, the wave fronts wheel as shown in Fig. 30 (*b*). (Compare this with Fig. 29 (*b*).)

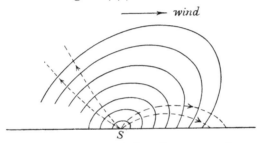

Fig. 31. The effect of a wind gradient on sound waves.

This accounts for the fact that audibility at ground level is better on a summer evening than during the day. Notice that sound does *not* travel more quickly in the evening but is refracted downwards instead of upwards as during the day.

(*b*) *Wind gradient.* The pealing of church bells is more audible when the wind is blowing towards us than when it is blowing away from us. This is another example of refraction, due to a wind gradient, in the atmosphere. For the wind near to the surface of the earth is always somewhat impeded, and hence the velocity of the wind increases with increasing height.

The sound waves are distorted as shown in Fig. 31. The tops of the waves move more rapidly, owing to the wind, than the lower parts. It will be seen that the sound rays travelling in the direction of the wind bend downwards and those travelling against the wind bend upwards.

This phenomenon was investigated by Professor Osborne Reynolds by means of an interesting experiment which you can perform for yourself. He placed an electric bell about 1 ft. above the ground and set it ringing. He wriggled full length along the ground into the wind, and at a distance of 20 yards from the bell he ceased to hear it. On raising his head he heard the bell again. At a distance of 30 yards the bell could not be heard 3 ft. above the ground, and at 70 yards, 6 ft. above the ground. At a greater distance even a pair of steps did not give sufficient height to hear the bell.

By means of the steps the sound could be heard for some distance to leeward of the bell and it was found to be stronger than at the same distance to windward. This fact, surprising at first sight, is due to the waves being lifted up, with the result that no sound energy is lost by friction with the ground.

The silent zone.

In January, 1917, a munitions factory blew up at Silvertown, London. The sound of the explosion was heard in the Home Counties and also in Lincolnshire and Norfolk, but no sound was heard in the intermediate region of Cambridge, Huntingdon and parts of Suffolk and Essex (see Fig. 32).

The effect is always observed when a loud noise such as an explosion occurs, and the intermediate region where no sound is heard is called the *silent zone*.

At many places in the region beyond the silent zone (i.e. Norfolk and Lincolnshire) double, triple, and even quadruple reports of the Silvertown explosion were heard. This must have been due to sound waves reaching this area by different routes, the later reports travelling a longer distance in the air.

The phenomenon can be accounted for by the refraction of sound owing to temperature or wind gradients (or both) in the atmosphere.

We know, for example, by sending up balloons, that the temperature of the atmosphere decreases up to a height of about 7 miles and then begins to increase. As a result of this reversal of the temperature gradient a sound ray could be bent as in Fig. 33. (Compare with Fig. 30 (*a*) and (*b*).)

This is probably not a complete explanation of the phenomenon. Wind gradients are bound to affect the path of the

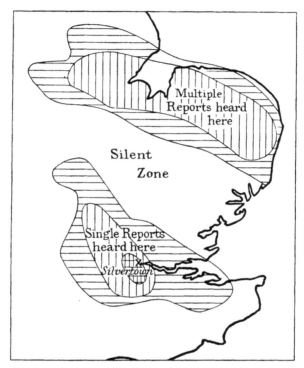

Fig. 32. The sounds heard of the Silvertown explosion. The shading gives some indication of loudness—horizontal shading representing least loud, and cross shading, loudest reports.

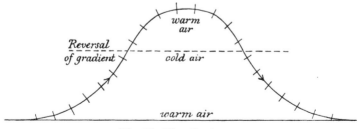

Fig. 33. The silent zone.

waves, and also the upper atmosphere may contain a high percentage of light gases such as hydrogen and helium, in which the velocity of sound is greater than in air.

The diffraction of sound.

We have already noted (see p. 41) an example of the diffraction of sound, i.e. the spreading of sound round corners. Owing to its long wave-length (which may be as large as 60 ft.) sound can bend easily round corners; it does cast sound shadows, however, if the obstacle is large enough.

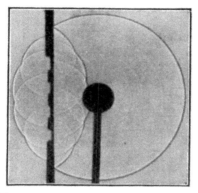

Fig. 34. The diffraction of a sound wave at a five-barred grating.

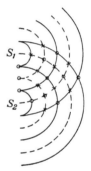

Fig. 35. Interference.

Fig. 34 is a photograph of the diffraction of sound at a five-barred grating. When a sound wave passes through a narrow aperture it spreads sideways as though the aperture were the source, of sound. Similarly, when it is reflected from a small obstacle, it spreads out with the obstacle as centre. It will be seen in the photograph that the separate transmitted waves have combined to form an almost perfect wave of large radius, as though there had been no obstacle. Similarly the reflected wave is almost the same as would have been obtained had there been no openings in the grating.

Interference.

In our study of light we have seen that, under certain conditions, two waves of light will annul each other and produce bands of darkness. In a similar way two sound waves may annul each other and produce bands of silence. The phenomenon is called *interference*.

In Fig. 35 S_1 and S_2 represent two sources generating sound waves. Each complete wave consists of a compression and a rarefaction, and the middle of a compression is represented by a continuous semi-circle and the middle of a rarefaction by a dotted semi-circle.

The two sets of waves pass through each other and where a compression and a rarefaction coincide in position, marked × in Fig. 35, they annul each other's effect, the air is quiescent, and there is silence. On the other hand, where two compressions or two rarefactions coincide, marked o in the figure, the resulting amplitude is the sum of the two separate amplitudes and the sound is correspondingly loud. It will be seen from the figure that there are alternate bands of silence and loudness and these are called interference bands.

These bands may be located experimentally by means of a sensitive flame. A jet of gas is allowed to pass through a fine nozzle in a drawn-out glass tube for example. The gas will burn in a tall quiet flame, until, on increasing the gas pressure, a critical stage is reached, beyond which the flame is short, broad and noisy. Below this critical pressure the flow of the gas is streamlined: above it, when the gas flares, the motion is turbulent.

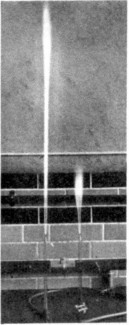

By courtesy of B. F. Brown, Esq.

Fig. 36. Sensitive flames. In silence, both are as tall as the one on the left, and during a hissing noise both duck like the one on the right. The photographs of the two flames were taken singly with separate exposures.

Sound waves, especially high-pitched sounds such as a hiss or the jingle of keys, cause a sensitive flame (with the gas just below the critical pressure) to flare. In Fig. 36 the short flame is flaring and the tall flame is not.

Interference may be demonstrated very simply with a vibrating tuning-fork (see Fig. 37). When the prongs move outwards they cause a compression to be sent out in the directions OA and OB, and simultaneously a rarefaction in the directions OC and OD; on moving inwards they send out a rarefaction in the directions OA and OB and a compression in the directions OC and OD.

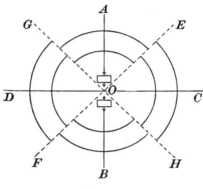

Fig. 37

Two sets of waves are therefore spreading out in the surrounding air, one set being half a period or wave-length out of phase with the other. Along the directions OE, OF, OG, OH the compressions of one set of waves and the rarefactions of the other will almost exactly coincide and there will be almost complete silence.

Thus if a vibrating fork is slowly rotated, with its stem as axis near to the ear, a sound of varying loudness is heard. The sound has a maximum intensity in the directions OA, OC, OB, and OD, and a minimum intensity in the directions OE, OH, OF, OG.

We shall meet several other examples of interference during the course of our study of sound.

SUMMARY

Sound may be *reflected* and obeys the same laws of reflection as light.

The acoustic properties of a room are investigated by determining the *reverberation time*, which is the time taken for a sound in the room to become inaudible.

Sound is *refracted* whenever it passes from one medium into another in which its velocity is different. It is therefore refracted when there is a temperature or wind gradient in the atmosphere.

Sound can spread round corners, a phenomenon called *diffraction*, but an obstacle which is large compared with the wavelength will cast a "sound shadow".

Two sets of sound waves may produce *interference*: where a compression and a rarefaction coincide the air is quiescent and there is silence.

QUESTIONS

1. Explain carefully, with special reference to the physical principles involved:

(a) A man at the top of a ladder can hear a man on the ground better than the man on the ground can hear him.

(b) Sounds in an empty house seem louder than when the house is furnished.

(c) The sound of distant church bells seems louder when the wind is blowing from them than when it is blowing towards them.

(d) Some pulpits are equipped with "sounding" boards.

(e) When walking past railings the noise of one's footsteps is often accompanied by a ringing sound.

2. During bomb practice in the neighbourhood of a corrugated fence an observer noticed that the explosion of each bomb was followed by a shrill echo. Explain this with a rough diagram of the relative positions of the bomb, the fence and the observer.   (L.)

3. Reproduce Fig. 22 on paper accurately to scale and verify that the "image" is as far behind the reflecting surface as the source of sound is in front. Draw two other positions of the incident and reflected waves a fraction of a second before and after the instant at which Fig. 22 was taken.

4. A sharp noise made in front of a regular flight of stairs produces a ringing echo. If the width of the tread of each step is 9 inches, find the pitch of the note.

5. Two umbrellas are opened, their covers wetted, and they are fixed with their handles towards each other and their sticks in the same straight line, at a distance of between 10 and 20 yards. If one boy places his ear near the stick and about 6 in. in front of one umbrella, he can hear clearly the ticking of a watch held in a similar position in front of the other umbrella. Explain carefully with a diagram why this is so. Why must the covers be wetted?

6. (a) What is the usual cause when the acoustics of a hall are unsatisfactory? If a speaker cannot be heard distinctly should he raise his voice? How may the acoustics be improved?

(b) Why does a given area of sound-absorbent material have (i) roughly the same effect whatever its position in a hall, (ii) a greater effect in a small hall than in a large one?

(c) From what other acoustic defect may a hall suffer besides excessive reverberation? How is this cured?

7. Explain carefully with the aid of diagrams why sounds are usually more audible at night than during the day.

8. Write a short account of the phenomenon known as the *silent zone*.

9. Describe an experiment to illustrate the refraction of sound. What determines the relative intensities of the refracted and reflected waves when sound passes from one medium to another?

10. Explain what is meant by the diffraction of sound. How is it that a band can be heard round a corner and yet cannot be seen? Under what conditions may a sound "shadow" be produced?

Fig. 38

11. Explain what is meant by the *interference* of sound.

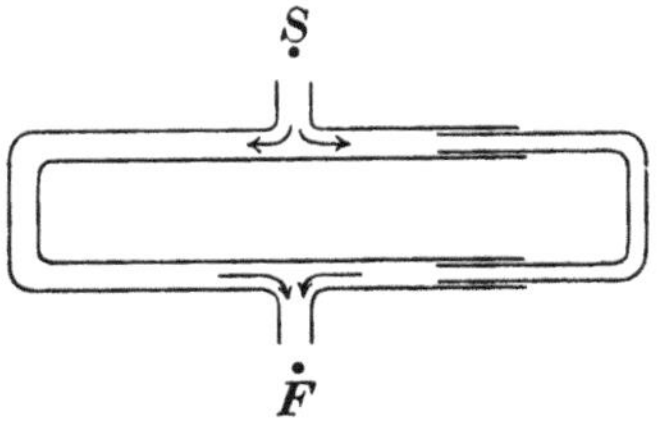

In Fig. 38 S represents a source of sound of high pitch and F a sensitive flame. The sound passes from S to F by two different routes shown by the arrows. Describe and explain the behaviour of the flame when the right-hand part of the tube is made to slide slowly in or out.

Chapter IV

MUSICAL NOTES. FREQUENCY

It is convenient to divide all sounds into two categories, (1) *musical notes*, which have a definite pitch, and (2) *noises*, which have no recognisable pitch.

A musical note has three characteristics, **pitch, loudness,** and **quality.** The pitches of the notes given out by a piano rise as we pass from the bass end of the keyboard to the treble. The loudness of the notes depends on the force with which we strike the keys. The quality of the notes is that which distinguishes them from notes of equal pitch and loudness sounded on a different instrument, e.g. a 'cello or a trumpet.

We naturally enquire what properties of a sound wave are responsible for these characteristics of a musical note.

Pitch and frequency.

The pitch of a note is determined and measured by the frequency of vibration of the particles in the sound wave, which is equal to the frequency of the source: the greater the number of vibrations per sec., the higher is the pitch. Fig. 39 represents traces on the same smoked plate of tuning-forks sounding notes of low and high pitch respectively.

The curves in Fig. 39 may also be used to represent the sound waves generated in the air by the tuning-forks. They are displacement diagrams.

Now sounds of all frequencies travel with the same velocity. Hence, although only one wave is sent out by one of the forks of Fig. 39 while the other sends out several, the disturbances travel equal distances in the same time. Thus the wave length, λ, of a sound of low pitch is longer than that of a sound of higher pitch.

Loudness.

The loudness of a sound depends on the energy of the particles in the sound wave which strike the ear-drum. If they are vibrating violently, i.e. with a large amplitude (see p. 2), they will

cause large changes of pressure on the ear-drum and a loud
sound will be heard. The note represented by the wave trace in
Fig. 39 (*a*) is louder than that in (*b*) since the amplitude is greater.

At the same time, in (*b*) more waves strike the ear-drum per second
than in (*a*): loudness depends on frequency as well as amplitude.
If the amplitude of (*b*) had been equal to that of (*a*), then (*b*) would
have been the louder. In broadcasting, when a powerful soprano
reaches her top notes, the engineers have to cut down the power to
prevent "blasting". There is never any such trouble with a bass.

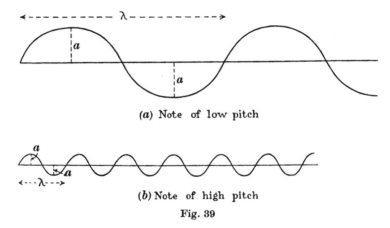

(*a*) Note of low pitch

(*b*) Note of high pitch

Fig. 39

Quality.

The characteristic quality of the note emitted by a musical
instrument is due to the fact that the note is not pure, but is a
blend of several notes of different frequencies and loudness. The
phenomenon is discussed in Chapters V, VI and VII.

Savart's toothed wheel and the siren.

The frequency of a note may be determined by means of
Savart's toothed wheel, shown in Fig. 40. The wheel is rotated
by an electric motor and a card is pressed lightly against the
teeth. The vibrations of the card give rise to a musical note. The
faster the rotation of the wheel the higher the note.

If we know the number of teeth on the wheel and measure its speed of rotation (by means of a revolution counter and a watch) we can calculate the rate of vibration of the card. For example, suppose that there are forty-eight evenly spaced teeth on the wheel, and that the latter is making ten revolutions per sec. The card is vibrating $48 \times 10 = 480$ times per sec.

In order to determine the frequency of a note given out, say by a tuning-fork, the speed of the motor is varied until the note given out by the card has the same pitch as that of the tuning-fork.

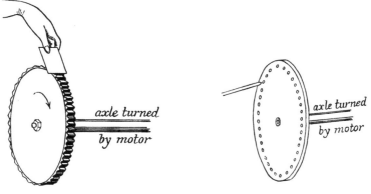

Fig. 40   Fig. 41. The siren.

A similar instrument, known as a siren, consists of a disc with evenly spaced holes round its circumference (see Fig. 41). A jet of air is blown against the holes while the disc is rotating. The frequency of the note produced is equal to the number of puffs emitted by the holes per sec., i.e. the product of the number of holes round the circumference of the disc and the number of revolutions per sec.

Fig. 42 shows a self-driven siren invented by Cagniard de la Tour. A fixed disc is situated below the revolving disc, and contains an equal number of holes. The holes are cut through the discs obliquely as shown in the figure, thus air, blown up from below, is slewed round on passing through them, thereby giving a push to the upper disc, and fulfilling the twofold function of driving the siren and generating the note. [The dual function of the air blast is open to the objection that it causes the low notes to be, of necessity, weak, and the high notes loud.] The speed of rotation may be controlled by varying the pressure of the air—a difficult operation. At the top are revolution counters.

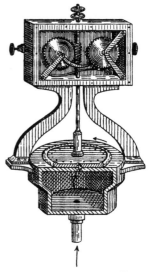

Limits of audibility.

The lowest note which can be distinguished by the average person has a frequency of about 20 c.p.s., while that of the highest audible note is about 20,000 c.p.s. These values vary considerably, however, for different people, and the range decreases with age. It has been suggested that the top notes in the songs of birds such as the blackbird are inaudible to most people owing to their high frequency. The frequencies of the notes used in music lie between about 30 and 5000 c.p.s.: above a frequency of 5000 the ear cannot distinguish difference in

Fig. 42. Cagniard de la Tour's siren.

pitch. The lowest and highest notes on a piano have frequencies of 27 and 3500 c.p.s. respectively.

Longitudinal waves with a frequency of 50,000 c.p.s. are used in submarine signalling. As these waves are above audible frequency they are called "ultra sonic" waves. Again, the "sounds" of explosions are sometimes of too low a frequency to be heard. They are called "infra-sonic" waves.

The analogy between such waves and ultra violet and infra red "light" is evident.

Determination of frequency by a wave-trace method.

The frequency of a tuning-fork may be determined by connecting a bristle to one of its prongs and causing it to make a wavy trace on a smoked glass disc, like a gramophone record, on a gramophone turn-table. The revolutions of the turn-table are timed with a stop-watch and the number of waves made by the tuning-fork in, say, exactly half a revolution, counted. Hence the number of vibrations made by the fork per sec. can be calculated.

Stroboscopic methods of determining frequency.

A stroboscope is a device for making a moving object appear at rest.

A rapidly rotating wheel, which is illuminated by intermittent flashes of light, will appear at rest if each spoke moves, during the interval between the flashes, into the exact position previously occupied by another spoke. If the spokes move either not quite so far or a little farther in the interval, the wheel will appear to be rotating slowly backwards or forwards respectively. So long as the flashes exceed about 16 per sec., owing to the persistence of vision, there will be no appearance of flicker.

It is evident that if the rate of the flashes can be both controlled and measured, the rate of rotation of the wheel may be determined.

The method is used for timing gramophone turn-tables. A paper disc with evenly spaced radial markings is illuminated by a neon lamp connected to alternating-current mains. A neon lamp glows red when an electric discharge at 180 volts or over is passed through the gas (neon) which it contains. (The red lamps used in illuminated advertisements are usually neon lamps.) The flash takes place at the instant the voltage is applied and ceases as soon as it is removed.

Now the electric current supplied by the "Grid" alternates at the rate of 50 c.p.s. In each cycle the voltage changes from, say, 0 to +230 and back to 0, 0 to −230 and back to 0. Hence a neon lamp connected to these mains will flash 100 times per sec. The rate of flashing in this case is known but not controllable.

Suppose the speed of rotation of a disc, containing eighty sectors, is increased until it appears at rest when illuminated by such a lamp. The disc must turn through $\frac{1}{80}$ revolution in $\frac{1}{100}$ sec. Hence the number of revolutions per minute made by the disc is $\frac{1}{80} \times 100 \times 60 = 75$. (If the speed of rotation of the disc is exactly doubled it will again appear at rest. Why?)

Stroboscopic methods are possible, and indeed were first employed, without the aid of a neon lamp. A vibrating body, such as a tuning-fork, may be viewed through a slit which is alternately opened and closed at a known rapid rate, by rotating vanes, or some other means. The rate of rotation of the vanes is adjusted until the vibrating body appears to be at rest.

Stroboscopic methods of various types are widely used, not only for determining frequencies but also for viewing and photographing moving machinery.

Beats.

When two notes of slightly different frequencies are sounded together the combined sound becomes periodically louder and softer. The effect is rather like a throbbing and the throbs are known as *beats*.

A simple way of demonstrating the phenomenon is to use two forks of the same frequency and reduce the frequency of one of them by loading its prongs with wax.

Consider, for simplicity, an observer who is equidistant from the two forks and suppose that the forks have frequencies of 100 and 101 c.p.s., respectively. When they both send out compressions together these compressions will arrive at the observer together, and he will hear a loud sound. After the lapse of $\frac{1}{2}$ sec. one fork will have made 50 complete vibrations and the other $50\frac{1}{2}$ vibrations, so that they are sending out, one a compression and the other a rarefaction. These reach the observer simultaneously, almost annul each other, and he hears practically no sound. After another $\frac{1}{2}$ sec. the forks are again sending out compressions simultaneously which arrive in step at the observer. Hence the beats occur at the rate of 1 per sec., the difference of the frequencies. *Similarly with forks of frequencies f_1 and f_2, there will be $f_2 - f_1$ beats per sec.*

The phenomenon is clearly an example of interference (see p. 47). It may be further explained with the aid of Fig. 43. The dotted curves represent the two sets of waves emitted by the forks: they have slightly different wave-lengths. The black continuous line represents the resultant sound, obtained by adding algebraically the displacements in the two waves. At first the two waves are in step and reinforce each other, but they become progressively more and more out of step until eventually the rarefactions due to one fork is "fitted" by the compression due to the other, when they almost annul each other.

The counting of beats is a very accurate method of determining the difference in frequency between two notes. It has been found possible to detect beats as slow as 1 in 30 sec., an accuracy in frequency difference of $\frac{1}{30}$ vibration per sec. Since electrically maintained tuning-forks are used for the accurate measurement of very short time intervals (to $\frac{1}{1000}$ sec.) the importance of the method in this connection is evident.

Scheibler made an instrument which he called a tonometer for measuring frequency by means of beats. It consisted of a set of sixty-five forks with frequencies from 256–512 (i.e. middle C to its octave), rising in stages of exactly 4 vibrations per sec. By counting the beats between a note and the notes of several of the forks, the unknown frequency of the note could be determined very accurately.

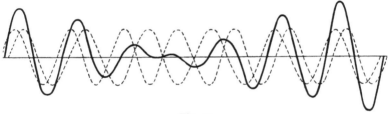

Fig. 43

The piano tuner utilises beats. He adjusts the tension of the string of middle C until there are no beats between the note it emits and that of a standard fork.

Beats can often be heard in the sound emitted by church bells. This is due to a lack of symmetry in the bell resulting in two concurrent vibrations. The tremulant effect of the voix céleste stop in the organ is produced by pairs of pipes, tuned to slightly different frequencies which cause slow beating.

The Doppler effect.

When a railway locomotive, sounding its whistle, approaches a station at speed, the apparent pitch of the note heard by a person on the platform is higher than the true pitch heard by the engine driver. When the locomotive passes the observer the apparent pitch falls suddenly and is lower than the correct pitch as the locomotive recedes. The effect was first discovered by Doppler and the earliest experiments were carried out with trumpets carried by locomotives.

Fig. 44 is a diagram to illustrate the cause of the phenomenon. *S* represents a source of sound, and *O* an observer. The dots represent compressions in the air sent out by *S* so that the distances between two dots represent complete wave lengths.

 Direction of sound

(a)

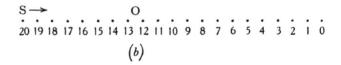

(b)

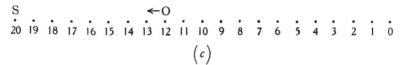

(c)

Fig. 44. Diagram to illustrate the Doppler effect. (a) Source and observer stationary. (b) Source moving towards observer. (c) Observer moving towards source.

Suppose, for simplicity, that *O* is exactly 10 wave-lengths from *S*. If both *S* and *O* are stationary, suppose *S* sends out exactly 20 compressions per sec., then the positions of the compressions after 1 sec. are shown in (a).

If however *S* has been moving towards *O* the positions of the compressions are those shown in (b). It will be seen that *O* has now received not 10 but $12\frac{1}{2}$ compressions (or more accurately wave-lengths) in the same time, $\frac{1}{2}$ sec. Hence the pitch of the note heard by *O* is higher than in case (a).

It will be seen from the diagram that we have assumed that S has moved 4 wave-lengths while sending out 20 compressions, i.e. in 1 sec. Hence each wave-length of the sound is only $\frac{16}{20}$ as long as in (a). Thus the number of compressions or wave-lengths received by O is

$$\frac{10}{\frac{16}{20}} = \frac{200}{16} = 12\frac{1}{2} \text{ in } \frac{1}{2} \text{ sec.}$$

Now let us suppose that S is stationary and that O moves towards S at the same speed as S was moving towards O in (b), i.e. 2 wave-lengths in $\frac{1}{2}$ sec. (see Fig. 44 (c)). It will be seen that O has now received 12 compressions in $\frac{1}{2}$ sec. and hence the pitch of the note heard by O has risen less than it did in (b).

How are we to account for the difference in the pitch of the note heard by O in (b) and (c)? The relative velocities of source and observer are equal in the two cases. It will be seen that in (b) the spacing of the compressions and therefore the wave-length of the note was altered by the motion of S. In (c), however, the wave-length of the note is unchanged.

Example 1. A railway locomotive has a whistle of frequency 800 c.p.s. What will be the pitch heard by an observer when the engine is approaching him, sounding its whistle, at 100 ft. per sec. (i.e. about 68 m.p.h.)?

The velocity of sound in air is 1100 ft. per sec. (It is a good plan to refer to Fig. 44 while trying to follow the solution.)

The whistle sends out 800 compressions per sec. In this time the first compression has travelled 1100 ft. but the engine has moved 100 ft.

Hence there are 800 compressions in the distance

$$1100 - 100 = 1000 \text{ ft.}$$

But in 1 sec. the compressions in a distance of 1100 ft. (the velocity of sound) must reach the observer. In 1100 ft. there must be

$$\frac{1100}{1000} \times 800$$

compressions. Hence pitch of note heard by observer

$$= \frac{1100}{1000} \times 800$$
$$= 880 \text{ c.p.s.}$$

Example 2. Suppose in Example 1 the stationary observer sounds a whistle of frequency 800. What will be the pitch of the note heard by a person on the train?

The number of compressions reaching a person on the train per sec. will be those contained in a distance $1100 + 100$ ft. Hence pitch of note heard $\frac{1200}{1100} \times 800 = 872\frac{8}{11}$ c.p.s.

An aeroplane capable of travelling faster than sound would provide interesting acoustical phenomena. The pitches of the sounds emitted by an approaching aeroplane moving nearly as fast as sound would be so high as to be inaudible. If the aeroplane travels exactly the speed of sound, the accumulated noises of a considerable period arrive simultaneously with the aeroplane. The resulting ear-splitting report might well prove dangerous. Suppose now that the aeroplane approaches at a speed greater than that of sound. All noises emitted by the aeroplane will be heard backwards—a similar effect, we must presume, to that obtained by running a gramophone record backwards.

The Doppler effect is observed with light as well as with sound and has great importance in astronomy. It is possible, for example, to calculate the speed with which distant stars are approaching or receding from us by the change in the wave-length of the light they send out. The method is to observe the shift in the lines in the spectrum.

SUMMARY

The frequency of vibration of a source of sound may be determined by (1) Savart's toothed wheel or the siren, (2) a stroboscopic method, (3) a wave-trace method (in the case of a tuning-fork).

When two notes of nearly equal frequencies are sounded together a periodic waxing and waning of the loudness of the combined sound is heard, known as *beats*. *The number of beats per second is equal to the difference in frequencies of the notes.* The phenomenon is an example of interference.

When a source of sound is travelling towards a stationary observer its apparent pitch is raised. When it passes the observer and recedes its apparent pitch is lowered suddenly. A similar effect occurs when the source is stationary and the observer moves, but the change of pitch is slightly different for the same relative velocity between source and observer. The phenomenon is known as the Doppler effect.

QUESTIONS

1. Explain:

(a) How Savart's toothed wheel may be used to find the frequency of a note.

(b) If there are two wheels on the same axle with the same number of teeth, but one wheel is larger than the other, what will be the difference in the notes they produce?

(c) What will be the effect on the note if the teeth are unevenly spaced or if teeth are missing?

2. Describe a simple siren and explain its use.   (O.)

3. How would you attempt to find in the laboratory the frequency of the hum emitted by an electric fan?   (O.)

4. A cog-wheel having 25 teeth is rotated 3 times per sec. and a thin strip of metal is fixed so that it is struck by the cogs. Assuming that the velocity of sound is 33,150 cm. per sec., what is the wave-length of the note emitted?   (O.)

5. A siren of the type shown in Fig. 42 having 36 holes round its circumference is blown round at a speed of 300 revolutions per min. (a) in air, (b) in water. What are the frequencies and wave-lengths of the notes it produces? Take the velocities of sound in air and water as 1100 and 4700 ft. per sec., respectively.

6. Describe two experiments by means of which you could show that the pitch of a note depends on the frequency of the vibrations causing it.

7. A bristle attached to the prong of a tuning-fork of frequency 256 makes a wavy trace consisting of 96 complete waves round exactly half the circumference of a smoked disc when the latter is rotated on a gramophone turn-table. Find the speed of rotation of the turn-table in revolutions per min.

8. Explain the principle of a stroboscopic method of finding the frequency of a vibrating body.

The vibrating prongs of a tuning-fork are viewed through a rotating disc which contains 50 evenly spaced radial slits. If the speed of the disc has to be increased to 240 revolutions per min. for the prongs to appear at rest, what is the frequency of the fork?

9. In order to find the frequency of a tuning-fork two strips of aluminium foil are attached to its prongs (see Fig. 45). In each strip of foil there is a slit and the slits are oppo-site each other when the prongs are not vibrating. A disc with 40 evenly spaced dots round its circumference is rotated by an electric motor, and is viewed through the slits when the fork is set vibrating. The speed of the motor is adjusted until the disc appears stationary. The disc is then turning at 420 revolutions per min. Calculate the frequency of the fork.

Fig. 45

At what speed of the motor will the disc appear to be revolving backwards at the rate of 1 revolution per sec.?

10. A smoked glass plate is held vertically by a piece of thread. A tuning-fork is clamped in such a position that a bristle attached to

one of its prongs just touches the plate. The tuning-fork is set vibrating by bowing it and the plate is allowed to fall by burning the thread. The waves in the trace made by the bristle on the plate become clearly separated at a distance of 4 cm. from the beginning of the trace. In the next 10 cm. there are exactly 12 complete waves. Find the frequency of the fork. (Acceleration due to gravity = 981 cm. per sec.^{2}.)

11. When two tuning-forks A and B are sounded together the intensity of the sound is found to increase and decrease periodically. Explain this with the aid of a diagram.

It is found that the sound dies away twice every second. If a little wax is put on the prong of fork B, the variations of intensity are found to occur more rapidly. If the frequency of fork A is 256 per sec., what is the frequency of fork B?

12. A car travelling at 30 m.p.h. sounding its horn of frequency 240 c.p.s. approaches a policeman. What are the apparent frequencies of the note to the policeman as the car approaches and recedes?

13. If in Question 12 the policeman had been producing a sound of frequency 240 c.p.s., what would have been the apparent frequency to the occupants of the car?

14. Two motor cars are approaching each other at speeds of 40 and 50 m.p.h. respectively. The horn of the first car is sounded and its note has a pitch of 100 c.p.s. What will be its apparent pitch to the driver of the second car?

15. Would you expect the velocity of the wind to have any effect on the apparent pitch of a note sounded at a distance in the open air? If so, would there be any difference when the wind is blowing (a) away from, (b) towards, the source of sound?

Chapter V

VIBRATIONS OF STRINGS

The transverse vibrations of strings constitute one of the chief sources of musical sounds. The piano, violin, and guitar represent three types of stringed instruments in which the strings are struck, bowed, and plucked respectively.

Take out the front of a piano and look at the strings. They are made of steel and stretched tightly on a cast-iron frame which is bolted to the sounding board. The bass strings are (1) longer, (2) thicker and more massive, being weighted with spirals of wire, (3) slacker than the treble strings.

This variation in the length, massiveness, and tension of the strings is a feature of all stringed instruments.

The violin has four strings made of catgut, tuned, by adjusting their tensions, to different notes (e^{II}, a^{I}, d^{I}, and g: see p. 115). The string of lowest pitch is covered with silver wire, to make it more massive. Each string may be made to produce notes of higher pitch by shortening its length: the violinist presses it with his finger some distance from the end.

The guitar has six strings, under different tensions, whose lengths may be varied in a manner similar to those of the violin. Three are made of catgut and three of silk covered with silver wire.

The sonometer.

It is evident, from our brief discussion of the piano, violin, and guitar, that the frequency of vibration, f, of a stretched string may be altered by changing, (1) its length, l, (2) its tension, T, (3) its mass per unit length, m.

We shall now consider how the exact relation between these quantities may be determined experimentally. The instrument we use is called the sonometer, or monochord.

It consists of a string, usually made of wire, attached at one end to a nail fixed to a board, and at the other end to a spring balance as in Fig. 46. The length of the wire can be varied by means of a movable bridge, *B*, and the tension by turning the wing nut, *S*. There is often a second wire stretched alongside for purposes of comparison.

1. *To find how* f *varies with* l (*keeping* T *and* m *constant*).

Several tuning-forks of different known frequencies are required. Adjust the tension of the wire to any suitable value at the beginning of the experiment and do not alter it.

Sound one of the forks and move the bridge *B* until the string when plucked gives out a note of the same frequency. When the notes are of nearly equal frequencies beats will be heard, and this is a help in making the adjustment.

Repeat the experiment with several forks. If the frequency is doubled it will be found that the length of wire must be halved, and so on.

Fig. 46. The sonometer. (This particular type, utilising a spring balance, was designed by Mr D. G. A. Dyson.)

Plot f against $\frac{1}{l}$. The resulting graph will be a straight line passing through the origin. What does this prove?

2. *To find how* f *varies with* T (*keeping* l *and* m *constant*).

Select a convenient length of the string and do not alter it during the experiment.

Tune the string to the forks by turning the wing nut, and read the tensions on the spring balance. It will be found that the tension must be quadrupled in order to double ($\sqrt{4}$), the frequency.

Plot f against $\sqrt{T}$. What kind of graph do you expect?

3. *To find how* f *varies with* m (*when* l *and* T *are constant*).

Obtain several strings of different thickness and find their mass per cm. length by weighing, or by measuring their diameter (knowing the density). Fix them in turn in the sonometer adjusting their tensions to be the same.

Since the possession of forks of the exact frequencies of the wires (at any given tension) is extremely unlikely, tune the wires to *one* fork by varying their lengths.

Plot l against $\sqrt{m}$. The graph will be found to be a straight line. Hence $l \propto \sqrt{m}$. But $f \propto \frac{1}{l}$. Therefore $f \propto \frac{1}{\sqrt{m}}$.

In this way it can be shown experimentally that

$$f \propto \frac{1}{l}, \quad f \propto \sqrt{T}, \quad f \propto \frac{1}{\sqrt{m}},$$

i.e.
$$f \propto \frac{1}{l}\sqrt{\frac{T}{m}}.$$

Now if f is measured in vibrations per sec., l in cm. (or ft.), T in dynes (or poundals), m in gm. per cm. (or lb. per ft.), it is found that

$$f = \frac{1}{2l}\sqrt{\frac{T}{m}}.$$

The reader should now interpret the facts about piano and violin strings, given on p. 63, in the light of this formula.

Quality and overtones.

The notes of a piano, violin and guitar each have a characteristic quality (see p. 51). What is it in the vibrations of their strings which causes this difference of quality?

When plucked at its mid-point a stretched string vibrates as in Fig. 47 (*a*) (backwards and forwards between the limiting positions shown), and emits a note which is called its *fundamental*. It is this note whose frequency is given by the equation

$$f = \frac{1}{2l}\sqrt{\frac{T}{m}}.$$

The string can vibrate in other ways, however. If it is bowed at a point a quarter of its length from one end, and at the same time touched lightly with a feather at its mid-point, it will vibrate as in Fig. 47 (*b*). The points marked N are stationary, and are called *nodes*: midway between them are points of maximum displacement called *antinodes*. The note given out has twice the frequency of the fundamental since the string is vibrating as though a bridge were placed at the middle and its length were halved. It is known as the *first overtone.*

Again, by bowing and touching at appropriate points the wire may be made to vibrate as in Fig. 47 (c), giving the second overtone. The frequency of this note is three times that of the fundamental. Similarly ten or more overtones may be obtained.

Now a string can vibrate in many of these ways simultaneously giving out all the notes corresponding to the modes of vibration. Thus if a string is plucked one quarter of its length from one end

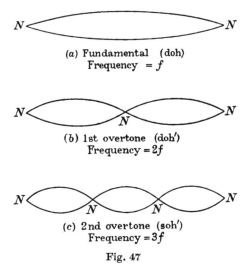

(a) Fundamental (doh)
Frequency $= f$

(b) 1st overtone (doh')
Frequency $= 2f$

(c) 2nd overtone (soh')
Frequency $= 3f$

Fig. 47

(and not touched at its centre), it will give out both its fundamental, which is heard most strongly, and also its first overtone, and other overtones as well.

The quality of the note given out by a string is determined by the number and relative intensities of the overtones, which depend on where and how the string is excited.

A piano string is struck by a padded hammer between one-seventh and one-ninth of its length from one end, causing the higher overtones up to the tenth to be quite strong. This gives a hard brilliant quality to the notes. Generally speaking the first five overtones give richness and fulness, while the higher overtones give brilliancy. The notes of piano strings are reinforced by a sounding board, without which they would be thin and weak.

The bowing of a violin string (at a point about one-seventh of its length from one end) enables the note to be sustained at will, and causes characteristic intensities of the various overtones. The quality of the note, however, is due mainly to the resonance of the body of the violin which selects and emphasises particular overtones. The shape, the nature of the wood and even the varnish of the body affect the quality. The most skilful maker of violins was Stradivarius, who lived in the seventeenth and eighteenth centuries, and a genuine "Strad" commands a high price. The piercing quality of a violin note is caused by the higher overtones, i.e. the fifth to the tenth.

A guitar string is plucked and hence its notes die away quickly. Particular overtones are reinforced by the body of the instrument as in the case of the violin.

Further examination of the modes of vibration of a stretched string.

We have seen that overtones are due to the remarkable fact that a stretched string may vibrate in two or more stationary loops (see Fig. 47), which appear to open and close, while a number of points along its length (the nodes, marked N) remain at rest.

The phenomenon may be produced very simply with a few yards of rope. Tie one end of the rope to a hook in a wall and hold the other end in the hand. Start moving the hand rhythmically up and down. At a certain speed of the hand the rope will vibrate in a single loop. On increasing the speed of the hand the rope may be made to vibrate in first two, then three, etc., loops.

A more convenient method of producing a large number of loops is to tie a string to an eccentric on the shaft of an electric motor, which replaces the moving hand. Hold the other end of the string. When the motor is switched on the string begins to vibrate in loops whose number may be varied by altering the pull on it by the hand.

A classic experiment of this kind was performed by Melde using, as vibrator, instead of the hand or motor, a tuning-fork (see **Fig. 48**). The tensions of the string were adjusted by placing weights in the scale pan until it vibrated in one, two, three, four, etc., loops when the fork was excited. These tensions were found to be in the ratio $16:9:4:1$ ($f \propto \sqrt{T}$).

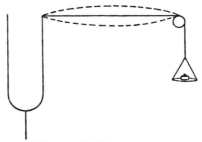

Fig. 48. Melde's experiment.

Stationary waves in a stretched string.

In the experiment we have just described, the vibrator is sending transverse waves along the rope or string. We do not, however, see waves passing along the string. The loops appear to be stationary and merely to open and close. We must enquire into the reason for this.

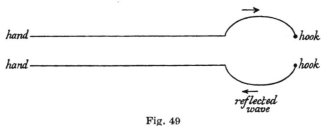

Fig. 49

Attach one end of a rope to a hook in the wall. Hold the other end in the hand, and by moving it sharply up cause a crest (or half of a wave) to travel along the rope. The crest will be reflected at the hook but will be reversed as shown in **Fig. 49** and will return along the rope as a trough.

This is known as a *reversal of phase* and is explained as follows. As the front of the disturbance travels along the rope, successive particles of the rope are pulled upwards, forming a new position of the crest. When the disturbance reaches the hook, however, the latter does not move. It is pulled upwards and reacts, pulling downwards on the rope with an equal and opposite force. (If it cannot pull downwards with an equal force it is wrenched out of the wall.) This downward pull of the hook sets up a reflected wave consisting of a trough which travels back along the rope.

Now when the hand, holding the rope, moves up and down rhythmically, it sends a series of waves (crests and troughs) down the rope. These give rise to reflected waves returning from the hook, and soon there are two sets of waves travelling in opposite directions along the rope. At most speeds of the hand these result in confusion, but at certain speeds their combined effect causes the rope to split up into loops (such as we have studied). These loops—*the resultant of two sets of waves of equal frequencies and amplitudes moving in opposite directions, are called stationary or standing waves.* They are clearly an example of interference (see p. 47).

We will consider in detail how they are formed. In Fig. 50 the thin continuous line represents the incident wave. It is continued beyond the hook. We have seen that the incident wave suffers a reversal of phase at the hook on becoming the reflected wave, i.e. a crest becomes a trough. Hence the reflected wave, represented by the dotted line, may be obtained by reversing (i.e. turning upside down) the incident wave continued beyond the hook and making it travel in the opposite direction. The thick black line is obtained by adding algebraically the displacements of the incident and reflected waves. It is thus their resultant, the stationary wave, and shows the actual position of the rope. The five cases represent different phases or positions of the incident wave, and the corresponding positions of the reflected and stationary waves. It will be seen that although the incident and reflected waves are passing along the rope the stationary wave stands still. It simply changes in amplitude. In cases 1 and 5 its amplitude is the sum of the amplitudes of the incident and reflected waves, since the latter are everywhere in phase. In case 3 the amplitudes of the incident and reflected waves are everywhere equal and opposite, thus annulling one another; the rope therefore occupies its undisturbed position.

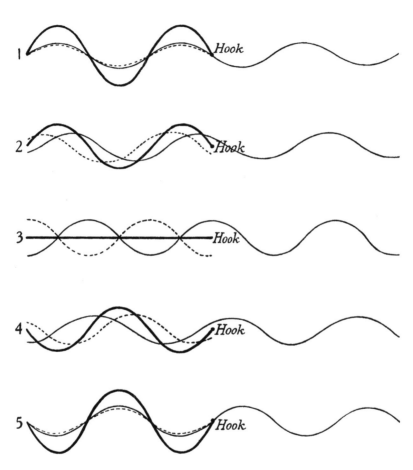

Fig. 50. Stationary wave in a stretched string. The thin continuous line represents the incident wave travelling from left to right, the dotted line the reflected wave travelling the opposite way, and the thick black line their resultant, i.e. the stationary wave. The position of the incident wave, had there been no hook and the rope had been twice as long, is drawn since the reflected wave is the reverse of this (i.e. turned upside down and going the opposite way). Five positions, or phases, of the waves are shown.

Final explanation of the modes of vibration of a stretched string.

We can now explain why a stretched string may be made to vibrate in a number of stationary loops, and also why it vibrates more quickly when the number of the loops is increased.

Two sets of transverse waves are set up in the string when plucked, which are reflected backwards and forwards at the two fixed ends. They combine to form stationary waves.

Their wave lengths, λ, are equal to the length of two loops, i.e. a crest and a trough. [Note that we are here dealing with the transverse waves in the wire and not the resulting sound waves.] Now $v=f\lambda$ (see p. 8), where v is the velocity with which the waves travel along the string (depending on its tension and mass per unit length), and f is the frequency of vibration of the string.

Hence $f=\dfrac{v}{\lambda}$. In this equation, if λ is made smaller and v is constant, f must increase. Thus, since v is the same for all wavelengths, the greater the number of loops and consequently the smaller their length $\left(=\dfrac{\lambda}{2}\right)$, the greater the frequency f.

Thus when a string splits up from one loop into two loops, the wave-length is halved: hence the string vibrates twice as quickly as before, giving out a note of double the frequency, called the *octave*.

Chladni's figures.

A metal plate is capable of vibrating in a large number of ways, and hence of giving rise, like a stretched string, to a fundamental and a series of overtones. A simple but beautiful method of demonstrating its different modes of vibration was devised by Chladni.

Sprinkle a layer of sand over a horizontal metal plate, screwed at its centre to a vertical rigid upright. Bow the plate at points marked A (see Figs. 51 and 52) and touch it lightly with the finger at points marked N. The sand sets itself in patterns, known as Chladni's figures. Taking different positions of A and N Chladni obtained over fifty figures with a square plate and over forty with a circular plate.

The lines along which the sand settles are called nodal lines. The sand is thrown from those parts of the plates which are vibrating most strongly to the comparatively quiescent portions, the nodal lines.

These experiments have a practical interest in connection with gongs and bells: the latter vibrate simultaneously in a number of ways similar to those shown by Chladni's figures, and thus give rise to composite musical sounds.

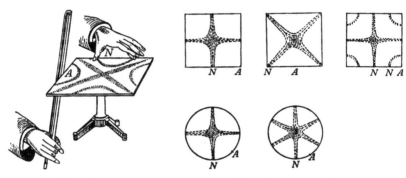

Fig. 51

Fig. 52. Chladni's figures.

SUMMARY

The frequency, f, of the fundamental emitted by a stretched string and the length, l, tension, T, and mass per unit length, m, of the string are related as follows:

$$f \propto \frac{1}{l}, \ f \propto \sqrt{T}, \ f \propto \frac{1}{\sqrt{m}}.$$

If these quantities are expressed in the correct units (see p. 65),

$$f = \frac{1}{2l} \sqrt{\frac{T}{m}}.$$

These relations may be verified experimentally by means of a sonometer.

A stretched string can vibrate in one, two, three or more loops. The points on the wire situated at the ends of the loops are stationary and are called **nodes**. The mid-points of the loops, where maximum displacement occurs, are called **antinodes**. When a wire is vibrating in one loop it gives out its **fundamental** (frequency f). When it is vibrating in two loops it gives out its **first overtone** (frequency $2f$). When it is vibrating in three loops it gives out its **second overtone** (frequency $3f$) and so on. A wire may vibrate in several ways simultaneously. The quality of the note it emits is determined by the number and relative intensities of the overtones.

The vibrations of stretched strings may be regarded as stationary waves. These are the resultant of two sets of waves setting out in opposite directions from the point where the wire is plucked and being reflected backwards and forwards at the ends of the wire.

The modes of vibration of a plate may be demonstrated by means of sand—Chladni's figures.

QUESTIONS

1. What do you understand by the frequency of a musical note? Explain how you would use a sonometer to prove that the frequency of vibration of a stretched string is proportional to the square root of the tension in the string.

The frequency of the fundamental note of a vibrating string is 300. With what frequency will a string of the same substance vibrate if the cross-section is doubled and the length halved, the tension remaining the same? (O.)

2. How can it be demonstrated that a tuning-fork and a sonometer are exactly in tune?

Given a sonometer and a single tuning-fork, and assuming that the frequency of the note emitted by a stretched string is inversely proportional to its length, how would you investigate the relation between the frequency and the stretching force on the wire? (C.)

3. What factors determine the frequency of vibration of a stretched string?

Two wires of the same material have lengths in the ratio 2:3. If their diameters are the same, what must be the ratio of their tensions for the shorter wire to give a note an octave higher than the longer? (C.)

4. On what does the frequency of the note emitted by a stretched string depend?

Compare the frequencies of the notes emitted by two sonometer wires, made of the same wire, stretched by forces of 5·76 kg. weight and 4 kg. weight respectively, the lengths of the wires being 50 cm. and 40 cm. respectively. What would be the effect on the frequencies of these wires if they were wrapped with a layer of very fine wire?   (N.)

5. A rather unmusical person wishes to tune a wire to the note of a tuning-fork. How can this be done by him?   (L.)

6. State what you know of the way in which a stretched string vibrates when it is bowed. Being supplied with two tuning-forks, the frequency of one of which is known, describe in detail the experiment you would carry out with a sonometer to determine the frequency of the second fork.   (L.)

7. Explain the principle on which a violin player "tunes" his strings, and then from each string can obtain a series of notes.   (L.)

8. Account for the fact that the pitch of stringed instruments, such as the violin, changes as the temperature of the room changes.
       (L.)

9. A stretched wire emits middle C when plucked. What will be the effect on the note produced if the wire is clamped at its middle point?   (L.)

10. What is a node and an antinode?
Describe an experiment to show their production on a stretched string, indicating where they would be expected.
A stretched string is made to vibrate with (a) its fundamental note, (b) its first overtone. If the frequency of the fundamental note is 300, calculate the wave-length of the note and of its first overtone. (Velocity of sound = 33,150 cm. per sec.)   (O.)

11. Describe how overtones are produced by a stretched string.
Explain why a stretched string, whose fundamental frequency is 250, may be excited by resonance by a fork of frequency 750.

12. Calculate the frequency of the third and fourth overtones given out by a stretched string whose fundamental is 240 c.p.s.

13. In Melde's experiment (see Fig. 48) if the fork is turned through an angle of 90° so that its prongs vibrate in a direction at right angles to the string, the number of loops is doubled. Explain, with the aid of diagrams.

14. A steel wire and a catgut string of the same length and stretched with the same force give the same note when plucked. If the density of steel is eight times that of catgut, what is the ratio of their diameters?   (L.)

15. When a load of 5 kg. is suspended from the end of the wire of a monochord it is found that 35 cm. of the wire gives a note of frequency 256. When the load is increased to 6 kg., find (a) the frequency given by the same length, (b) the length required to give the same frequency. (L.)

16. A wire 1 metre long stretched by a force of 50 lb. gives a note of frequency 256. A bridge is placed $33\frac{1}{3}$ cm. from one end. What must the stretching force be made so that the longer segment gives a note of 256? (L.)

17. A stretched wire A vibrates in unison with 85 cm. of another wire B and a third wire C is in unison with 68 cm. of B. How must the tension on A be altered to make it vibrate in unison with C? (L.)

18. Two stretched strings emit fundamentals of frequencies 200 and 402 c.p.s. respectively. When they are plucked simultaneously beats are heard. Explain fully.

19. Describe briefly how the modes of vibration of a metal plate may be investigated. Explain, with the aid of diagrams, some of the ways in which a square plate can vibrate.

Chapter VI

RESONANCE. VIBRATIONS OF
AIR COLUMNS

When a vibrating tuning-fork is held in the air the sound it generates is feeble. If, however, its stem is placed on a table, the sound is much louder. The vibrations of the fork are communicated to the table top, which is able to set far more air in vibration than the prongs of the fork alone.

The vibrations of the table top are called **forced vibrations**, and their frequency is equal to the "forcing" frequency of the fork.

The sounding board of a piano provides a similar example. A wire hung from the ceiling and stretched taut by a weight gives out a feeble sound when plucked. But if the same wire is stretched between two nails on a board the sound is much louder, owing to the vibration communicated via the board to the air.

Forced vibrations and resonance.

The phenomenon of forced vibrations may be investigated by the following experiment devised by the late Professor Barton. A number of simple pendulums of slightly differing lengths (see Fig. 53), and having bobs consisting of small paper cones, are suspended from a stretched horizontal cord. Attached to the

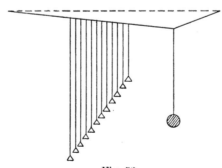

Fig. 53

same cord is another pendulum with a massive iron bob and of
length equal to that of the middle pendulum of the series.

When the massive pendulum is set vibrating its motion is
transmitted via the cord to the other pendulums. The latter
execute forced vibrations: they vibrate with the same frequency
as the massive pendulum and not with their own.

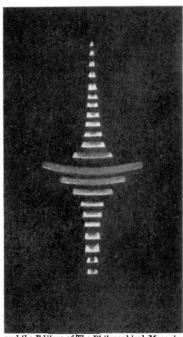

(a)   (b)

Fig. 54. Photographs of the paths of the bobs of the pendulums in Fig. 53,
when the pendulums are executing forced vibrations (a) heavily damped,
(b) lightly damped.

All the pendulums vibrate with almost equal amplitudes as
shown by the photograph in Fig. 54 (a), taken from the left-hand

side of Fig. 53. The broad white lines are caused by the moving bobs and represent their paths.

Owing to the light weight of the paper bobs these pendulums will not vibrate for very long if set vibrating on their own. Their vibrations die away rapidly and they are said to be heavily *damped*.

If curtain rings are now slipped over the paper cones, thereby considerably increasing the weights of the bobs, the pendulums become slightly damped. Their vibrations persist for a much longer time when they are vibrating freely, since the weight of the bobs is now considerably greater than the air resistance, which remains approximately the same as before.

The forced vibrations of the lightly damped pendulums are shown in Fig. 54 (*b*). Only that pendulum which has the same length, and hence the same natural frequency as the massive pendulum, acquires a large amplitude of swing.

The particular case of forced vibrations when the natural frequency of the body undergoing the forced vibrations is equal to that of the forcing vibrations is known as **resonance**.

Examples of resonance.

Soldiers marching over a suspension bridge always break step lest the period of vibration of their marching should coincide with that of the bridge. The cumulative effect of a considerable number of impulses applied at exactly the right instants might cause dangerously large oscillations of the bridge.

When we "tune" a wireless receiver, we are merely adjusting its natural frequency or wave-length, to that of the incoming wireless carrier waves, when it will be excited by resonance.

Again, when the "loud" pedal of a piano is depressed (thereby taking the dampers off the strings), and a note is sung loudly, some of the strings will be found to be "resounding". These vibrating strings have a natural frequency (that of the fundamental or of one of the overtones), which is exactly equal to the frequency of the air vibrations of which the sung note is comprised.

The resonant vibration of an air column.

Sound a tuning-fork over a glass cylinder or tall tumbler and slowly pour in water. When the air column above the water has been reduced to a certain length, it will be found to boom out or resound the note of the tuning-fork. The natural frequency of the air column is then equal to the frequency of the tuning-fork.

The celebrated tenor, Caruso, is said to have diverted himself after dinner by singing loudly the note to which the air in a wine glass resounded, causing such violent resonance that the glass was shivered into fragments.

A tuning-fork is often provided with a resonator consisting of a hollow wooden box (see Fig. 55), the air in which has the same period of vibration as that of the fork. The intensity of the sound generated, when the fork is struck, is thereby much increased. The duration of the sound will, however, be shorter since the resonator provides no extra energy, but merely causes the energy of the fork to be radiated more rapidly.

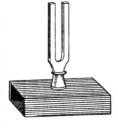

Fig. 55

Determination of the velocity of sound by a resonant air column.

The velocity of sound in air may be determined by measuring the length, l, of an air column which resounds strongly to a fork of known frequency, f. The length of the air column is adjusted by some such method as that indicated in Fig. 56 (a).

Now $v=f\lambda$ (see p. 8), where v is the velocity of sound and λ is the wave-length of the note; it can be shown (as follows), that $l=\dfrac{\lambda}{4}$.

When the lower prong of the tuning-fork moves from a to b (see Fig. 56 (b)) it sends out a compression. Suppose by the time it has finished sending out this compression, i.e. when it has reached b and is beginning to move back from b to a, the front of the compression has travelled down the tube, been reflected at the bottom and just reached the top of the tube again. In moving from b to a the prong assists the compression out of the tube—by making way for it, and causes a rarefaction to travel down the tube. When the prong reaches a this rarefaction will just have travelled down and up the tube. The prong, in moving from a to b again, now sends another compression down the tube, and so the cycle is repeated. It is clear that, under these circumstances, resonance will occur since the fork is delivering perfectly timed impulses to the air in the tube.

Thus the disturbance travels down the tube and up again while the fork executes exactly half a vibration (from a to b or b to a). This distance must therefore be half the wave-length, λ, of the sound generated: thus the length of the tube is $\dfrac{\lambda}{4}$.

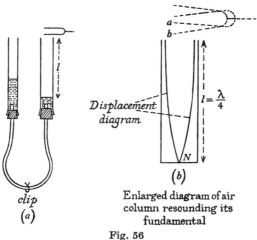

(b)

Enlarged diagram of air column resounding its fundamental

Fig. 56

Since the air just above the tube takes part in the vibration an end correction of $0\cdot6r$ (where $r=$ the radius of the tube) must be added to the length of the tube.

Thus
$$l+0\cdot6r=\frac{\lambda}{4}.$$

The following is a set of readings from an actual experiment:

	Frequency of fork	$=256$ c.p.s.
	Length of resounding air column	$=31\cdot75$ cm.
	Radius of tube	$=2\cdot5$ cm.
$\therefore$	Wave-length of note	$=4\,(31\cdot75+0\cdot6\times2\cdot5)$
		$=133$ cm.

But
$$v=f\lambda.$$
$\therefore$ Velocity of sound $=256\times133=34{,}000$ cm. per sec.

Since the velocity of sound increases with temperature, the value of the latter should be recorded. In the above experiment, it was 15° C. The velocity at 0° C. can be calculated from the formula given on p. 18.

Mode of vibration of an air column.

In Fig. 56 (b) the vibration of the air column is represented by a displacement diagram. We shall see (p. 82) that this is really a stationary wave. The whole air column may be regarded as vibrating up and down rather like a spring held at one end—concertina-wise: it is evident that the air at the closed end of the tube cannot move, whereas that at the open end vibrates longitudinally through the largest amplitude (with a frequency equal to that of the fork). There is thus a node—a position of zero displacement, N, at the closed end, and an antinode—a position of maximum displacement at the open end. This way of looking at the phenomenon, and in particular, the displacement diagram, again elucidates the fact that the length of the air column is one-quarter the length of a wave.

The note emitted by the air column, when it vibrates in this way, is called its *fundamental*.

Resonance of the first overtone.

Can an air column, like a stretched string, vibrate in more than one way? If the air is contained in a tube closed at one end and open at the other (as in the experiment just described), any form of vibration must clearly be subject to the condition that there must be a node at the closed end and an antinode at the open end.

Fig. 57 shows a manner of vibration which fulfils this condition. In this case the wave-length is only one-third of that in Fig. 56, and hence the frequency is three times as great.

That the air column is capable of vibrating in this manner may be proved experimentally as follows. Sound over the tube a fork of frequency three times the value required to cause resonance of the fundamental. The air column resounds, though not so strongly as before. The note is called the *first overtone*.

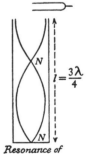

$l = \dfrac{3\lambda}{4}$

Resonance of first overtone

Fig. 57

We shall see that numerous other overtones are also possible. Draw the displacement diagram for the second overtone

$$\left(l = \frac{5\lambda}{4}\right).$$

The need for applying an end correction in the resonance experiment for finding the velocity of sound (see p. 80) may be obviated by the following method:

After finding the length l when the air column is resounding its fundamental, increase the length about three times and then carefully adjust it until the air column resounds its first overtone, using the same fork (see Fig. 58). Measure this length, which we will call l'.

Now $\qquad\qquad\dfrac{\lambda}{4} = l + 0\cdot6r \quad$ (see p. 80),

and $\qquad\qquad\dfrac{3\lambda}{4} = l' + 0\cdot6r.$

Subtracting, $\qquad\qquad\dfrac{\lambda}{2} = l' - l.$

Hence $\qquad\qquad v = f \times 2\,(l' - l).$

Stationary waves in air.

The longitudinal vibrations of air columns bear striking resemblances to the transverse vibrations of strings. This is due to the fact that both may be regarded as stationary waves.

Thus, in the experiment we have just described, the fork is sending down the tube a continuous series of waves, while a continuous series of reflected waves is simultaneously passing up the tube. When two trains of waves of equal frequency and amplitude are passing in opposite directions, stationary waves result.

The way in which the air layers vibrate in stationary waves is represented in Fig. 58. At the top of the diagram successive positions of the displacement diagram (see p. 13) are shown. These are numbered 1, 2, 3, 4, etc., in their correct sequence.

The horizontal lines of little men, also numbered 1, 2, 3, 4, etc., correspond respectively with the identically numbered position of the displacement diagram. The men are all given a letter, A, B, C, D, etc., and correspond to layers of air.

It will be seen that A, E, I, M never move. They are situated at nodes.

C, G, K move faster and farther than the rest. They are situated at antinodes. Their amplitudes are represented in the displacement diagram by the greatest width of the "loops".

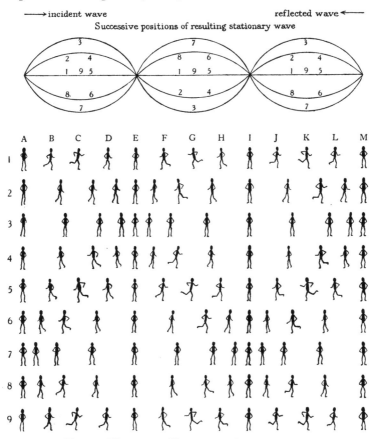

Fig. 58. Diagram to illustrate stationary waves.

The remainder of the men (or air layers) have an intermediate amplitude.

It is of interest to compare Fig. 58 with Fig. 10 on p. 11. Note that in a stationary wave the air layers do not vibrate in succession as in an ordinary longitudinal wave: they all vibrate together. Thus in lines 3 and 7 all are stationary, while in lines 1, 5 and 9 they are all moving through their undisturbed positions at their maximum speeds.

Note also how at the nodes the men alternately bunch up and separate. Thus, although the layer of air at a node suffers no displacement, there is a maximum pressure change there. On the other hand, at an antinode, although there is maximum displacement, the pressure remains comparatively constant and normal.

The stationary wave in the resonant air column sounding its fundamental (see Fig. 56 (*b*)), is represented by men *C, D, E* in Fig. 58. *C* represents the antinode at the top of the air column and *E* the node at the bottom.

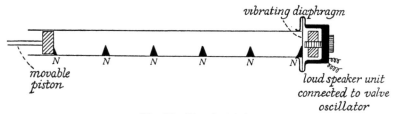

Fig. 59. The dust tube.

When the air column is sounding its first overtone (see Fig. 57), the wave is represented by men *C* to *I* in Fig. 58.

The manner in which transverse stationary waves are caused by the resultant effect of trains of incident and reflected waves was shown in Fig. 50. A similar argument to that given on p. 69 applies alike to longitudinal as to transverse waves.

However, when a longitudinal wave is reflected at the closed end of a tube there is no reversal of phase. A compression is reflected as a compression and a rarefaction as a rarefaction.

On the other hand, reflection may take place at the open end of a tube, and in this case a compression is reflected as a rarefaction and *vice versa*. Thus there is a reversal of phase in this case. When it reaches the open end, a compression overshoots the end of the tube, leaving a rarefaction which travels back down the tube.

Kundt's dust tube.

Stationary waves in a gas contained in a glass tube may be rendered "visible" by placing a light powder such as cork dust or lycopodium powder in the tube. The powder collects in heaps at the nodes since it is buffeted away from the antinodes, where the displacement of the gas is a maximum. The method was devised by Kundt.

Fig. 59 shows a tube with a loudspeaker unit, connected to a valve oscillator at one end, and a movable piston at the other. The loudspeaker sounds a note of constant frequency, and the position of the piston is adjusted until the powder, contained in the tube, collects in heaps as shown in the figure. Since the tube is closed at both ends, there must be nodes at the ends, and stationary waves will be set up only when the effective length of the tube is a whole number of half wave-lengths of the note emitted by the loudspeaker. The experiment is exactly analogous to Melde's experiment with a tuning-fork and a stretched string (see Fig. 48).

The wave-length, λ, in the gas in the tube may be measured since it is equal to twice the distance between two adjacent nodes. If the frequency, f, of the note is known, the velocity of sound, v, in the gas may be calculated from the formula $v = f\lambda$. This is a convenient method of finding the velocity of sound in gases.

If the intensity of the note emitted by the loudspeaker is high, the powder in the tube, besides collecting in heaps at the nodes, splits up into striations and also rises in sharp discs at the antinodes (see Fig. 60). The explanation of this phenomenon is beyond the scope of this book, but it is mentioned because the distance between the antinodal discs can be measured much more accurately than that between the nodal heaps. In this way the wave-length can be determined to 1 part in 1000.

In the original form of Kundt's tube the exciting note was emitted, not by a loudspeaker but by the

By courtesy of Prof. N. A. da C. Andrade

Fig. 60. The phenomena of the dust tube when the latter is excited by a note of high intensity. The bright discs of powder are situated at the antinodes: midway between them are the nodes.

longitudinal vibrations of a glass or metal rod (see Fig. 61), clamped at its centre and carrying a light plate which fits into the tube. The rod is made to vibrate by stroking it with a wet cloth; the movement of the plate sets up waves in the gas in the tube.

With this apparatus, knowing the velocity of sound in the gas, it is possible to determine the velocity in the solid substance of which the exciting rod is composed.

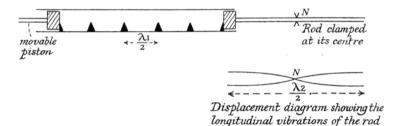

movable piston

Rod clamped at its centre

Displacement diagram showing the longitudinal vibrations of the rod

Fig. 61

Suppose

v_1 = velocity of sound in the gas,

v_2 = velocity of sound in the solid,

λ_1 = wave-length of note of frequency f in the gas,

λ_2 = wave-length of note of frequency f in the solid.

Then
$$v_1 = f\lambda_1,$$
$$v_2 = f\lambda_2,$$
$$\frac{v_2}{v_1} = \frac{f\lambda_2}{f\lambda_1} = \frac{\lambda_2}{\lambda_1}.$$

To determine v_2, knowing v_1, it is therefore necessary to find λ and λ_2.

Now the rod is clamped at its centre but is free to move longitudinally at both ends. It will therefore vibrate in the manner shown in the displacement diagram in Fig. 61, having a node at its centre and antinodes at both ends. The wave-length, λ_2, is clearly equal to twice the length of the rod.

The wave-length in the gas, λ_1, is (as we have already shown) equal to twice the distance between the nodal heaps of powder. Hence v_2 can be calculated.

Wind instruments.

Organ pipes. The organ is a wind instrument comprising a whole orchestra of pipes, in which the air vibrates in a manner similar to that we have described.

By courtesy of Henry Willis and Sons, Ltd.

Fig. 62. Some of the pipes of the organ of St George's Hall, Liverpool. The tall pipes bent over at the top are reed pipes. Immediately behind them is a row of stopped (or closed) flue pipes. In front of them there is a row of flue pipes, each of which has a hole near the top and a movable band: this is for tuning purposes. The flue pipes at the top of the picture are diapasons: they have a full rich tone and form the basis of all organ music.

Fig. 62 shows some of the pipes of the organ in St George's Hall, Liverpool. The pipes are arranged in groups at right angles to

88 SOUND

the gangway. Each group includes as many pipes as there are keys in the keyboard—short to long pipes, ranging from treble to bass, and each set of pipes has its own characteristic shape or type, so that its notes have a different quality from the rest.

Suppose that two stops on an organ are pulled out and a key is depressed. Wind is blown into two pipes causing them to

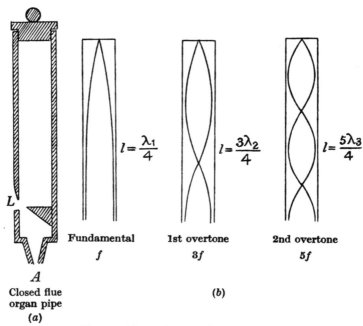

Fundamental
f

1st overtone
$3f$

2nd overtone
$5f$

L

A
Closed flue organ pipe
(a)

(b)

Fig. 63. Notes given out by a closed pipe.

"speak", and two notes having the same pitch but different quality are sounded together.

There are two main types of organ pipes: (1) flue pipes, (2) reed pipes.

(1) *Flue pipes.* Figs. 63(a) and 64(a) represent closed and open flue pipes respectively: the former has been drawn as a wooden

pipe with a rectangular cross-section and the latter as a metal pipe with a circular cross-section.

Wind from the organ bellows passes into the pipe at A and strikes the sharp edge, or lip, L. The impact of the air stream on the air in the pipe sets the latter vibrating in a manner similar to that of the resonant air column described on p. 79. The air

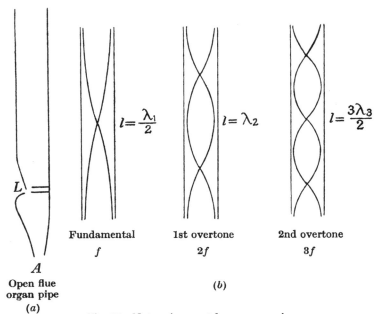

Fundamental   1st overtone   2nd overtone
    f $2f$ $3f$

$l = \dfrac{\lambda_1}{2}$ $l = \lambda_2$ $l = \dfrac{3\lambda_3}{2}$

L

A

Open flue
organ pipe
(a)

(b)

Fig. 64. Notes given out by an open pipe.

stream is forced alternately in and out of the pipe by the vibrations of the air column in the pipe with a frequency equal to the natural frequency of the air column.

The fundamental and first two overtones of a closed pipe are represented in Fig. 63 (b). The different possible modes of vibration are all subject to the condition that there must be a node at the closed upper end and an antinode at the lower end, which is (effectively) open.

It is apparent from the diagrams that the length of the tube is $\frac{\lambda_1}{4}$, $\frac{3\lambda_2}{4}$ and $\frac{5\lambda_2}{4}$, in the three cases respectively, where λ_1, λ_2, λ_3 represent the wave-lengths of the notes emitted. Hence, if f is the frequency of the fundamental, the frequencies of the overtones are $3f$, $5f$ and so on. These form the odd members of the harmonic series, f, $2f$, $3f$, $4f$, etc. (see p. 98).

The modes of vibration in an open pipe are shown in Fig. 64 (*b*). Here there must be antinodes at both ends, since both ends are open. The relation between the length of the tube and the wave-length of the notes is shown in the figure. If f is the frequency of the fundamental, the frequencies of the overtones are $2f$, $3f$ and so on. It is clear these, with the fundamental, form a complete harmonic series. Hence the quality of the note given out by an open pipe is different from that given out by a closed pipe.

Again the wave-length of the fundamental of an open pipe is half the wave-length of the fundamental of a closed pipe of equal length. Hence the frequency of the former is twice the frequency of the latter. When an open pipe is closed, therefore, its fundamental drops by an octave.

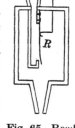

(2) *Reed pipes.* A reed pipe is shown in Fig. 65. The pitch of the note given out is governed mainly by the frequency of the reed, R, which is made to vibrate by the wind from the organ bellows. The pipe, P, serves mainly to bring out specific overtones by resonance. The pipe is tuned by moving the wire, W, which presses against the upper end of the reed.

Two types of reeds are used: (1) beating reeds, which are longer than and overlap the aperture they cover (as in Fig. 65), and (2) free reeds, which are shorter than the aperture. The former are used almost exclusively in organ pipes, but the latter are

Fig. 65. Reed pipe.

used in mouth-organs and harmoniums where there are no pipes to modify the quality of the notes emitted, since the notes given out by a beating reed are harsh.

The reader should take an old mouth-organ to pieces and examine its reeds.

Further wind instruments.

(1) *The tin-whistle.* The tin-whistle is an open flue pipe whose effective length can be varied by covering finger holes (see Fig. 66). The blast of air from the mouth strikes the edge or lip, *L,* and when all the holes are covered the whistle emits its lowest note. The positions of the holes are arranged so that as they are uncovered successively the notes of the diatonic scale are emitted.

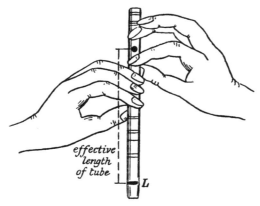

Fig. 66. The tin-whistle.

(2) *Wood-wind.* The wood-wind instruments of the orchestra comprise the *flute* (see Fig. 67), which is excited like a flue organ pipe—a blade-like stream of air being blown across an aperture, and the *oboe, clarinet* and *bassoon,* which are excited by small single or double cane reeds in the mouthpieces (see Fig. 68). All these instruments are provided with holes, some of which are covered by keys and the rest by the fingers.

(3) *Brass-wind.* Some brass-wind instruments are shown in Fig. 67. The lips of the player act as a double reed and set up the vibrations in the pipes of these instruments.

In the *bugle* there is no mechanism whereby the length of the tube may be varied. Hence different notes can be produced from it only by blowing overtones.

The *French horn* and *cornet,* in common with a number of other

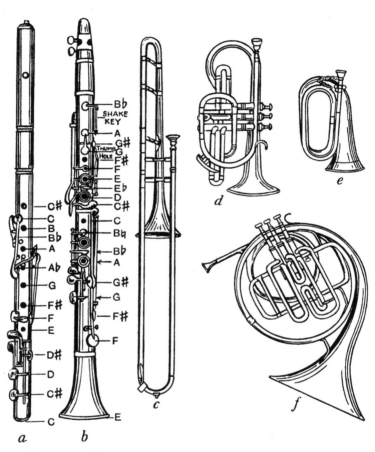

Fig. 67. *a*, Flute; *b*, clarinet; *c*, trombone; *d*, cornet; *e*, bugle;
f, French horn.

instruments, possess valves (or pistons) which, when depressed, add an extra length of tubing to the instrument and hence lower the pitch of the note emitted.

The length of the tube of a *trombone*, on the other hand, may be varied by moving in or out a **U**-shaped slide.

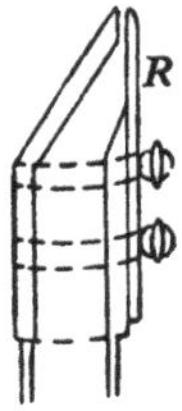

The human voice.

The voice is caused by a blast of air from the lungs setting in vibration two membranes called the vocal cords, between which there is a narrow adjustable slit called the glottis. The vocal cords are situated in the larynx or windpipe, the passage from the mouth to the lungs (see Fig. 69).

Fig. 68

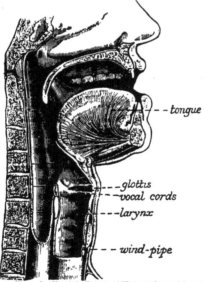

From Guillemin's Forces of Nature, *by courtesy of*
Messrs Macmillan and Co. Ltd.

Fig. 69

Helmholtz put forward the theory that the pitch of the voice depends on the tension, and hence the frequency of vibration of the vocal cords, and the quality on the shapes of the two resonant air chambers, the mouth and the pharynx (the passage from the mouth to the gullet and wind pipe), which emphasise certain overtones. This theory is supported by the fact that the vocal cords of men are 1·5 times as long as those of women, and that tenors have shorter vocal cords than basses, since the shorter a stretched membrane, the higher its frequency.

When different vowels are spoken at the same pitch, we do not alter the tension of our vocal cords but merely the shape of the mouth and position of the tongue. We alter thereby the notes to which the mouth and pharynx cavities resound, and hence the quality of the resultant sound emitted. Sir Richard Paget has made models with plasticine of the different shapes which these resonant chambers assume, and has been able to reproduce with striking faithfulness the various vowel sounds.

Most consonants, such as t, p, k, s, are generated without the aid of the vocal cords and are called unvoiced sounds.

Summary

A heavily damped body (one whose free vibrations die away rapidly) may be made to execute **forced vibrations** whose frequency is always equal to the forcing frequency. If, however, the body is lightly damped, it will respond appreciably only to vibrations of frequency equal to its own natural frequency. This particular case of forced vibrations, i.e. **the sympathetic vibration of a body caused by vibrations of the same frequency as its natural frequency,** is called **resonance.**

The wave-length of the fundamental of a (longitudinally) vibrating air column in a tube closed at one end is equal approximately to four times the length of the tube. More accurately

$$\frac{\lambda}{4} = l + 0 \cdot 6r \quad \text{(see p. 80).}$$

The velocity of sound in air may be determined by adjusting the length of such an air column until it resounds with a fork of known frequency, f. Then

$$v = f\lambda = 4f(l + 0 \cdot 6r).$$

Air columns can vibrate in a number of ways like stretched strings. At the open end (or ends) of a tube there must be an antinode, i.e. a position of maximum displacement, and at the closed end a node, i.e. a position of zero displacement. The fundamental and first two overtones of closed and open tubes are represented in Figs. 63 and 64.

The vibrations of air columns are stationary waves, the resultant of two sets of waves travelling in opposite directions in the tube. In wind instruments one set of waves is sent down the tube by blowing across a sharp edge by a vibrating reed, and the second set consists of the original waves reflected at the farther (open or closed) end. When compressional waves are reflected out of the open end of a tube there is a reversal of phase, but at a closed end there is no reversal of phase.

By means of Kundt's tube the wave-lengths of the stationary waves in a gas may be measured. The method is employed to determine the velocity of sound in (1) gases, (2) solids.

QUESTIONS

1. Describe and explain what is heard when a bottle is filled with water at a tap. (L.)

2. Explain carefully how the note, obtained by blowing across the open shank of a key, is generated. Why is this note of higher pitch than the "roaring" of a chimney on a windy day?

3. The level of water in a glass tube (diameter 5·0 cm.) is adjusted until the air column above the water resounds strongly the note of a tuning-fork of frequency 240 c.p.s. The length of the air column is 33·5 cm. Calculate the velocity of sound in air.

4. Two cardboard tubes, open at both ends, are of such diameters that one can just slide inside the other. The length of the combined tube is adjusted until it resounds the note of a fork of frequency 512 c.p.s. Calculate the velocity of sound in air, given that the length of the resounding tube is 30·8 cm. and that the average radius of the tubes is 4·0 cm. (Apply corrections for both ends.)

5. Explain what is meant by resonance, giving two examples. Calculate approximately the length of the resonance box, closed at one end, suitable for a tuning-fork of frequency 384. The velocity of sound in air may be taken as 1120 ft. per sec. (L.)

6. A long vertical brass tube, open at the top, contains water, the level of which can be adjusted. Explain carefully how the air in the tube can be set into resonant vibration by means of a tuning-fork.

When a fork of frequency 512 is sounded the difference in level of the water between two successive positions of resonance is found to be 33 cm. What is the velocity of sound in air? (N.)

7. Explain the phenomenon of the resonance tube. A vertical tube, 1 metre long, is filled with water which is allowed to run out gradually from the bottom. For how many positions of the water surface will it be possible to obtain resonance with a tuning-fork of frequency 512? The velocity of sound in air may be taken as 330 metres per sec. (C.)

8. Describe an experiment to show that the wave-length of a musical note in air is inversely proportional to its frequency. (L.)

9. (a) The frequency of the fundamental of an open organ pipe is 128 c.p.s. What are the frequencies of its first three overtones?

(b) If the pipe is closed at one end, what are now the frequencies of its fundamental and first three overtones?

10. What are the causes of *pitch* and *tone* (*quality*) of a musical note?
Two 4 ft. organ pipes, one closed at one end and the other open at both ends, are sounded on a day when the speed of sound in air is 1120 ft. per sec. Calculate the frequency of the fundamental note in each case. (N.)

11. Draw the displacement curves representing the fundamental and first overtone of a pipe open at both ends. In Fig. 58 what men can be taken to represent the air layers in these two modes of vibration? How do the various air layers vibrate?

12. An organ pipe when blown softly emits a note of frequency 192. When blown more strongly it emits a note of frequency 384. Is it a closed or an open pipe and what is its length? (The velocity of sound is 340 metres per sec.)

13. What effect would you expect change of temperature to produce on the pitch of musical wind instruments? Explain fully. (L.)

14. An organ pipe of effective length 25 cm. is stopped at one end. Calculate the wave-length and frequency of the note emitted by it when blown with air. What difference, if any, would you expect to find if carbon dioxide were substituted for air? The velocity of sound in air is 340 metres per sec. and the density of carbon dioxide is 1·44 times that of air. (C.)

15. The velocity of sound in hydrogen is 4200 ft. per sec. Find the length of a pipe open at both ends and filled with hydrogen, which will resound the note emitted by a fork of frequency 384. (Ignore end corrections.)

16. What do you understand by a *harmonic*, a *node*, and an *anti-node*?

Describe with explanations how you would demonstrate the production of these in the laboratory?   (O.)

17. Explain how sound is produced and what determines its pitch, loudness and quality in each of the musical instruments shown on p. 92.

18. What do you understand by resonance? Describe experiments you would make in the laboratory to show under what conditions resonance occurs.

Explain how a singer is able to produce notes of different pitch, amplitude and quality?   (O.)

19. A Kundt's tube such as is shown in Fig. 61 is filled with air and the exciting note is generated by stroking a glass rod 1 metre long, clamped at its centre. The distance between adjacent nodal heaps of powder in the tube is 13·6 cm. If the velocity of sound in the air is 340 metres per sec., find the velocity of longitudinal sound waves in the glass of the rod.

20. A brass rod 6 ft. long and clamped at its centre is made to vibrate longitudinally by stroking. If the note emitted has a frequency of 390 c.p.s., find the velocity of sound in brass.

Chapter VII

ANALYSIS AND RECORDING OF SOUND

Harmonics.

We have seen that the quality of a musical note is determined by the relative intensities of the various overtones which accompany the fundamental.

Suppose a source of sound is emitting a fundamental note and an overtone which is the octave of the fundamental, but of less intensity—represented by the dotted displacement diagrams in Fig. 70. The resultant sound is represented by the continuous displacement curve, obtained by adding algebraically the displacements in the dotted curves.

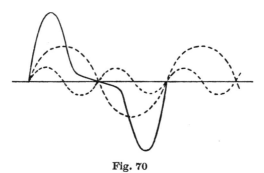

Fig. 70

The dotted curves are of the simple harmonic type (see p. 2), but the continuous curve is not.

Several types of apparatus now exist which enable us to examine sounds of different quality by obtaining their displacement curves (corresponding to the continuous curve in Fig. 70). We can then find the constituent simple harmonic components (corresponding to the dotted curves in Fig. 70) of which they are composed, either by calculation or by elaborate mechanical analysers specially invented for the purpose.

That this is always possible may be proved mathematically. Fourier, the great French mathematician, discovered a theorem stating that any periodic disturbance can be represented by a series of simple harmonic vibrations with frequencies in the ratios 1:2:3:4:5, etc., and of suitable amplitude, called *harmonics*.

Apparently the ear acts as a harmonic analyser. When a sound wave similar to that represented by the continuous curve in Fig. 70 falls upon it, the ear can detect its constituents—the dotted simple harmonic curves. This fact was expressed by Ohm (the discoverer of the well-known law in electricity) in what is known as Ohm's Law: "The ear recognises only simple harmonic vibrations as pure musical tones. It can resolve more complex vibrations into their simple harmonic constituents."

The eye is not so skilful. When lights of two different colours, e.g. red and green, enter the eye simultaneously, the eye sees one colour only—yellow.

Instruments for obtaining the wave forms of sounds.

The simplest type of instrument for making a photographic record of the wave form or displacement diagram of a sound is the *phonodeik*, invented by D. C. Miller (see Fig. 71).

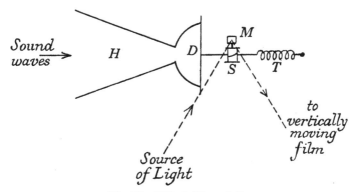

Fig. 71. Miller's Phonodeik.

The sound is collected by a horn, *H*, and impinges on to a very thin glass diaphragm, *D*. To the middle of the diaphragm is

attached a fine wire passing round a loose spindle, S, and kept
taut by a weak spring, T. Fixed to the spindle is a tiny mirror,
M, about 1 sq. mm. in area. The vibrations of the diaphragm
cause the spindle and mirror to rotate slightly. A beam of light,
reflected from the mirror on to a vertically moving film, is therefore deflected horizontally backwards and forwards and hence
makes a wave trace on the moving film.

The wave forms shown in Figs. 72 and 74 were taken by a boy
with a home-made instrument in which the sound waves were first
converted into varying electric currents by means of a carbon

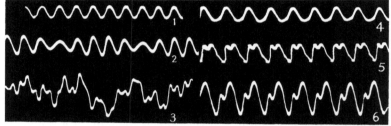

By courtesy of J. W. Findlay, Esq.

Fig. 72. Oscillograms showing the wave forms of different sounds: 1, tuning
fork; 2, beats between two tuning forks (512 and 426·6 c.p.s.); 3, a noise
caused by the tuning fork hitting the microphone; 4 and 5, organ pipe
blown softly and hard, respectively; 6, 18 in. open organ pipe.

microphone: the electric currents were magnified by a three-
valve amplifier and then made to rock a tiny mirror (corresponding to M in Fig. 71) attached to the armature of a loud-speaker
unit. The electrical method is more delicate than the mechanical
method utilised in the phonodeik, since the vibrations are amplified.

Wave filters.

Another method of examining the quality of sounds has been
developed in the Bell Telephone Laboratories. The sound waves
are picked up by a telephone and converted into corresponding
varying electric currents. By means of electric filters (which we
cannot explain here) currents corresponding to any desired fre-

quencies may be eliminated. The currents are converted back into sound by means of a loudspeaker.

In this way, sounds of the same pitch produced by, say, a piano, 'cello, and French horn may have all their overtones eliminated. The fundamentals are found to be almost indistinguishable.

Again, the fundamentals of these sounds may be eliminated, and then, successively, certain of the overtones. It is found that the higher overtones are more important in the notes of the piano and 'cello than of the French horn.

A very interesting phenomenon is illustrated by these experiments. When the fundamental and even, also, many of the lower overtones are eliminated, the ear still distinguishes the pitch of the note as that of the missing fundamental. In fact, the ear detects a frequency which is not there. Our ears had plenty of practice in such fabrication of the fundamentals of bass notes in the early days of gramophones and wireless loudspeakers: for a small horn will not reproduce the lowest bass notes of music. Again, the cost of large, expensive, bass organ pipes is sometimes avoided by providing instead smaller pipes which sound the appropriate overtones, thereby deceiving the ear into the impression that the fundamental is sounding.

Helmholtz resonators.

The experimental methods of investigating quality which we have just described are of comparatively recent date. The subject was investigated thoroughly in the middle of the nineteenth century by Helmholtz, with the aid of very selective air resonators. Each resonator was shaped like a turnip, with a small open neck, N (see Fig. 73), and a still smaller aperture or "pip", E, which was inserted into (or connected by means of a tube to) the ear.

Fig. 73

Owing to its small neck such a resonator does not radiate much energy: it does not loudly resound. As a result the vibrations in the air inside it persist for a considerable time. Thus it is lightly damped, and highly selective.

By means of a series of such resonators Helmholtz was able to pick out the overtones in sounds and estimate their relative strengths. In this way he analysed sounds.

He then proceeded to synthesise the sounds, i.e. reproduce them by sounding their constituents at the correct intensities. He did this by means of a series of electrically maintained tuning-forks placed in front of their corresponding resonators. The intensity of each component sound could be adjusted by varying the distance between the fork and the resonator, and also by partially closing the neck of the latter.

Speech.

Helmholtz investigated speech and the quality of vowel sounds. Consonants are noises rather than musical sounds, but vowels are complex musical sounds differing in quality because of the

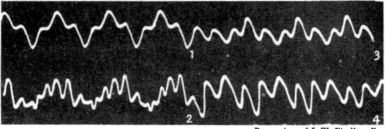

By courtesy of J. W. Findlay, Esq.

Fig. 74. Oscillograms showing the wave forms of different vowels: 1, *ee* as in "street"; 2, *ah* as in "father"; 3, *oo* as in "choose"; 4, *oh* as in "hope".

different intensities of the respective overtones. In Fig. 74 are shown oscillograms of different vowels. The shapes of the oscillograms are characteristic of each vowel sound and vary only slightly with different individuals. Even when the pitch is different, the shape of each complex curve is the same, although its wave-length, of course, is different.

The gramophone.

A bristle attached to a prong of a vibrating tuning-fork will produce a wavy trace on a smoked glass plate moved under it (see p. 3). If, when the fork has stopped vibrating, the experiment could be reversed, i.e. the plate moved back and the bristle made to move in accordance with the trace (by grooving the trace), the fork would be set vibrating again. This is the principle of the gramophone.

Fig. 75. A magnified photograph of the grooves of a gramophone record. The sound is generated by the sideways vibration of the needle as it is made to move along these grooves.

Fig. 76. A magnified photograph of a worn gramophone needle. Such a needle tends to ride up and down in the grooves of a record and cause excessive record wear.

By courtesy of The Gramophone Company

Fig. 77. A hydraulic press for making gramophone records. Note the nickel-plated copper negatives at the top and the bottom. The "record biscuit material" is warmed, stamped, and then cooled by cold water while in the press.

We have seen, in the earlier part of this chapter, how an instrument like a phonodeik can make a "trace" of any sound on a moving photographic film or plate. For reproduction by a gramophone the trace is produced by a cutting stylus on a wax disc, in the form of a wavy spiral groove. The stylus vibrates from side to side under the influence of the sounds being recorded, and hence cuts a wavy instead of a true spiral.

In the old mechanical method of recording, the stylus was connected direct to a diaphragm at the narrow end of a horn, and the only energy available for cutting the groove was that of the sound waves setting the diaphragm in vibration. Hence the performers were obliged to place themselves as near to the horn as possible.

The mechanical method, however, has now been superseded by the method of electrical recording. The sounds fall on a microphone (of the condenser type) and are thereby converted into correspondingly varying electric currents: these are amplified by valve amplifiers, and then, by means of an electromagnet, operate the cutting stylus. As much energy as is required for cutting may be supplied by the batteries feeding the amplifier. Another advantage of the method is that the microphone may be placed in a concert hall while the record is made at the gramophone company's headquarters, to which the currents set up in the microphone are transmitted by wires.

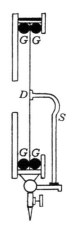

From the soft wax disc cut by the stylus, a nickel-plated copper negative is made (by electrolysis). This is fixed in a hydraulic press and used for manufacturing records by stamping its impression on "record biscuit material" (see Fig. 77).

The gramophone sound-box.

The apparatus which reproduces the sound from a record is called the gramophone sound-box. It consists (see Fig. 78) of a thin mica diaphragm, D, mounted between rubber "gaskets", G, and connected by means of a stylus bar, S, to a needle. When the needle vibrates sideways as it follows the

Fig. 78. Gramophone sound box.

deviations of the groove, the stylus rod turns about its pivot and moves the diaphragm backwards and forwards, thus producing pressure variations in the air similar to the original sound waves.

For pure reproduction the diaphragm should behave like a piston, alternately compressing and rarefying the air near to it, and ought not to vibrate in any of its natural frequencies (such as can be demonstrated by Chladni's figures, p. 72). To achieve this, as far as possible, the diaphragm is often connected to the stylus rod by a number of feet known as a "spider" instead of in the middle only.

The horn.

The sound produced by an unaided sound-box is weak, and it is made louder by the use of a horn. For many years after the introduction of the horn no one could give a satisfactory explanation of how it worked. It is believed now that its function, roughly, is to give the diaphragm more air to work on: the horn holds the air near to the diaphragm, and forces it to suffer compression by preventing it from escaping.

If the horn is made long and narrow it confines a large volume of air to suffer compression under the action of the diaphragm, but there is considerable reflection of the sound waves set up at the open end of the horn. On the other hand, if the open end is made wide, the sound can get out of the horn but it is not loud, since there is room for the air to move away from the diaphragm without suffering much compression.

The best shape for the horn is found to be an exponential surface. If the distance along the axis from the diaphragm is divided into units, then the areas of cross-section at these points, in an exponential horn, are in the ratio $1:2:3:4:5$, etc., respectively.

Now the diameter of the aperture of a horn must be at least one-quarter of the wave-length of the lowest bass notes it is required to reproduce, since otherwise these sounds will be unable to leave the tube owing to reflection. A wide aperture necessitates a long horn if it is of the exponential type. Hence in order that they may be long, and yet not take up too much room, horns are often folded as shown in Fig. 79.

Fig. 79. Folded gramophone horns.

Fig. 80. Berliner's gramophone (1894).

History of the gramophone.

The original ancestor of the gramophone was invented by Edison in 1877. The same instrument was used both for recording and reproducing the sound. It consisted of a membrane, to which was attached a stylus (or needle) and a horn. When sound waves fell upon the membrane it vibrated and caused the stylus to make an indented groove of varying depth in a sheet of tinfoil or waxed paper wrapped round a cylinder which was rotated by hand.

Then Bell introduced two improvements. He made the cylinders of wax and used two machines, one for recording and one for reproduction. Later, Edison conceived the idea of making electrotype replicas of each original record.

In 1894 Berliner began to make records in their modern form— discs with a spiral groove having sideways deviations. Gramophones at this time were turned either by hand or by foot: soon clockwork motors were introduced. The H.M.V. "Dog model" appearing in the famous picture used as a trademark, was brought out in 1899.

A recent development has been the radio-gramophone (a machine that can also be used for radio-reception). Here the vibrations of the needle, as it traverses the groove in a record, are converted by means of an electric pick-up (in place of the usual sound-box) into varying electric currents. These currents are amplified by a valve amplifier, such as is used in a wireless set, and then converted into sound by a loudspeaker.

Talking films.

The sound of the original talking films was recorded on gramophone discs which were carefully synchronised with the film. The disadvantages of this method were that the records deteriorated and were easily damaged, and also that if by some mischance, such as the jumping of the gramophone needle over a groove, the synchronisation were deranged, the sound and projection remained out of step for the rest of the reel.

The method now employed is a "sound track" down the side of the film. There are two types of sound track, (a) variable area, (b) variable density (see Fig. 81).

In both methods of recording, the sound falls upon a sensitive microphone which converts it into tiny varying electric currents corresponding to the sounds. These currents are amplified by a valve amplifier and are then passed, in the first method, through a delicate mirror galvanometer, the mirror of which is caused to vibrate in a manner corresponding to the vibrations of the original sounds. A narrow but intense beam of light is reflected by the mirror and falls upon the side of the film which is moving steadily: a track similar to that shown in Fig. 81 (a) is thereby produced.

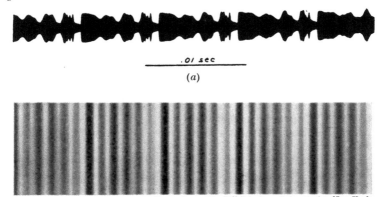

.01 sec

(a)

By courtesy of the Bell Telephone Laboratories New York

(b)

Fig. 81. Film sound tracks: (a) variable area, (b) variable density.

In the variable density method, the oscillating current from the amplifier, instead of being passed through a mirror galvanometer, is made to modulate the brightness of the light from a neon tube. The light is passed through a slit 0·0005 in. wide on to the moving film, and produces bars of varying density and distance apart (for sounds of varying pitch), on the film (see Fig. 81 (b)).

The sound track is arranged to be $14\frac{1}{2}$ in. in advance of the pictures in order that the sound-reproducing apparatus, or "sound head", may be below the "gate" of the projection apparatus.

The same sound head is used with both types of sound track.

The film is drawn steadily in front of a narrow slit illuminated by a powerful lamp. Light passes through the slit and the film and falls upon a photo-electric cell. Now when light falls upon a photo-electric cell a small electric current is produced whose size is proportional to the intensity of the light falling upon the cell (see the author's *Light*). Hence, as the film is drawn past the slit, variable electric currents corresponding to the varying density or width of the sound track are generated. These currents are amplified and carried by wires to loudspeakers placed behind the screen.

SUMMARY

The wave form or displacement diagram of a sound may be obtained by an instrument such as a phonodeik. The wave form of a musical or periodic sound may then be resolved mathematically into *harmonics*, a series of simple harmonic vibrations (each giving rise to a pure note with frequencies in the ratio 1:2:3:4:5, etc.), and of suitable amplitudes.

The constituents of a sound may also be examined by the use of wave filters or Helmholtz resonators.

Sound is recorded by imprinting (*a*) its wave form on a gramophone disc, (*b*) a trace corresponding to its wave form on a "talking" film.

QUESTIONS

1. Describe an instrument for producing the wave form (or displacement diagram) of a sound. What kind of wave forms would you expect in the case of sounds produced by a tuning-fork, a musical instrument such as a violin, and a book falling on the floor?

2. Write a short account of the way in which sound is recorded on a gramophone disc and how it is reproduced by a sound-box.

3. Describe the appearance of the groove on a gramophone record when the music is (*a*) loud, (*b*) soft, (*c*) of high pitch, (*d*) of low pitch. Why must a gramophone be run at the correct speed?

Chapter VIII

THE EAR. MUSICAL SCALES.
SCALES OF LOUDNESS

The ear.

The ear is divided into three compartments: (1) *the outer ear*, which serves as a channel to direct sound waves into the ear; (2) *the middle ear*, which takes up the vibrations of the sound waves, and magnifies the variations in pressure; (3) *the inner ear* or *labyrinth* (so called from its complicated shape), which responds to the pressure variations and sends the appropriate nerve stimuli to the brain.

The outer ear consists of the exterior and purely decorative appendage which we wear on the outside of our heads, called the *pinna*, and a passage of length between 2 and 2½ cm., closed by the *ear drum* or tympanum. Many animals can move their outer ears enabling them to collect and locate the direction of sounds, but man no longer possesses this power.

The middle ear is divided from the outer ear by the ear drum, see Fig. 82: this is a stretched membrane which vibrates when sound waves fall upon it.

A compound lever consisting of three bones is connected at one end to the ear drum and at the other to an oval membrane, called the *oval window*, which acts as a kind of window to the inner ear. The vibrations of the ear drum are communicated by this lever to the inner ear. The three bones forming the lever are called the *hammer*, the *anvil*, and the *stirrup*, names which are suggested by their shapes. Their arrangement is such that they reduce the motion communicated from the ear drum to the oval window, but increase the force between thirty and sixty times. The chamber of the middle ear is connected to the throat by a tube called the *Eustachian tube*. This enables air to pass in or out of the middle ear, and so adjust its pressure to that of the atmosphere. Gunners open their mouths, as in a yawn, at the moment of firing, to effect communication between the mouth and the middle ear through this tube. For the intense pressure wave set up by the explosion may rupture the ear drum if it falls on one side of it only.

The inner ear is extremely complex and we can give only a simplified account of it. Behind the oval window is a passage called the *vestibule* containing fluid and connected to the real organ of hearing, the *cochlea*, so called because of its resemblance to a snail shell. (The semicircular canals marked in Fig. 82 play no part in the sensation of hearing. They enable us to experience a sense of balance, and the giddiness we feel after continuously revolving is caused by the movement of the liquid in these canals.)

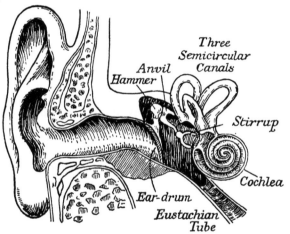

Fig. 82. The ear.

The cochlea consists of a spiral tube in the bone of two and a half turns, filled with fluid: stretched across the middle of it and coiling down its entire length is a membrane, called the *basilar membrane*, to which are attached nerves connected to the brain. This membrane has been taken out and uncoiled: it is found to be about 3 cm. long, 0·16 mm. wide at one end, and 0·52 mm. wide at the other. It is made up of a large number of fibres stretched across its width and kept in tension, and may be compared to a harp. The fibres are connected by nerves to the brain.

Vibrations, set up by sound waves, in the ear drum are communicated via the three bones of the middle ear to the oval window, and thence through the fluid in the cochlea to the basilar membrane. According to the resonance theory of hearing developed mainly by Helmholtz, only those fibres in the basilar membrane which have the same frequency as the incoming sound waves, are set in vibration by resonance. The fibres which are vibrating each cause a nerve current to be sent to the brain.

One of the objections to the resonance theory of hearing is that there is not sufficient difference in the lengths of the fibres in the basilar membrane to account for the large range of frequencies to which the ear is susceptible.

Now we know that the frequency of vibration of a stretched fibre is given by the equation $f = \dfrac{1}{2l} \sqrt{\dfrac{T}{m}}$ (see p. 65). The frequency depends not only on the length but also on the tension and mass per unit length of the fibre.

It has been suggested that the tensions of the shorter fibres are greater than those of the longer fibres, which would result in a much greater difference in frequency than would be the case if the tensions were all equal. Again, although the fibres do not differ appreciably in cross-section, it is assumed that the longer fibres are "loaded" with fluid more than the shorter ones, owing to the peculiar shape and arrangement of the cochlea. We have mentioned earlier that the long bass strings of a piano are "loaded" by means of spirals of wire for a similar reason, i.e. to reduce their frequency.

The resonance theory of hearing, which is obviously largely conjecture, is not universally accepted. There are a number of facts which support it, however. Workmen who are subjected to continual loud noises suffer from what is known as "boilermaker's deafness". They become deaf to sounds of certain pitch. This is neatly accounted for on the resonance theory by assuming that the fibres in the basilar membrane corresponding to these notes become damaged or atrophied. The ears of guinea-pigs which have been subjected to loud and continuous sounds of different pitch have been examined, and degeneration in the basilar membrane in positions to be expected on the theory have been detected.

A rival to the resonance theory is the "telephonic" theory which postulates that hearing does not take place by resonance at all. It is suggested that the basilar membrane vibrates as a whole, and that the brain distinguishes between notes of different pitch because the actual nerve currents have the same frequency as the sound. On the resonance theory, the sensation of pitch depends on which nerve transmits a current to the brain.

Musical intervals and scales.

Musical intervals. We have seen, in Chapter IV, that the pitch of a note is determined by its frequency. We shall now consider in greater detail the relation between pitch and frequency.

If four Savart's toothed wheels (see p. 52), on the same axle, are made to rotate together, and the number of teeth on these wheels are in the ratio 4:5:6:8, they will give rise to the notes "doh, me, soh, doh¹". If the speed of rotation is increased the pitches of all the notes rise but they still have the same pitch relation, "doh, me, soh, doh¹".

This illustrates a remarkable fact about the relation between pitch and frequency. A musical interval, such as the octave ("doh" to "doh¹"), is determined by the *ratio* of the frequencies of the two notes and not their difference. For the octave this ratio is 2:1.

Thus the frequencies of octave notes on a piano, as we pass from the bass to the treble, increase *not* by constant additions but in a constant ratio, 2:1.

An ordinary piano keyboard comprises six octaves. Let us consider the seven notes C and assume that the piano is tuned to scientific pitch, i.e. middle C has a frequency of 256. The following are the frequencies of these seven notes:

C_1	C	c	c^l	c^{ll}	c^{lll}	c^{llll}
32	64	128	256	512	1024	2048

Note that the frequencies of adjacent notes are in the ratio 2:1. But the difference in the frequencies of the bottom two notes is 32, while that for the top two notes is 1024. Yet these intervals seem so similar to the ear that they are called by the same name—an octave.

The diatonic scale. The diatonic scale, "doh, ray, me, fah, soh, lah, te, doh¹ ᵐ is familiar to everyone since it is the basis of European music. It is by no means the only musical scale in use, as all who have listened to Oriental music are well aware. But we shall confine our attention here to it alone.

The scale may be written out in staff notation as in Fig. 83 (a) and the notes are labelled with the first seven letters of the alphabet. The letters recur in each octave. Middle C is usually written c¹, its upper octave c¹¹, and its lower octave C, the same

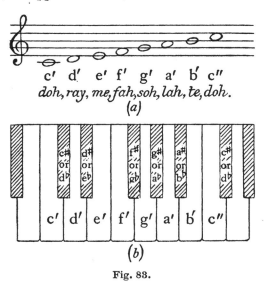

Fig. 83.

convention being used for the other notes. The keys on a piano corresponding to these notes are shown in Fig. 83 (b). By starting the scale with c¹ instead of a¹, only the white keys are used. We shall consider the use of the black keys later.

We have seen that the ratio of the frequencies of two notes which form an octave, e.g. c¹¹ and c¹, is 2:1. Now in the diatonic scale there are seven notes and hence seven in each octave. It might be expected that each of these seven intervals, i.e. the ratio of the frequency of each note to that of its predecessor, would be the same. But this is by no means the case. Taking C as 1, the ratios of the frequencies of the notes in an octave are:

C	D	E	F	G	A	B	C
1	$\frac{9}{8}$	$\frac{5}{4}$	$\frac{4}{3}$	$\frac{3}{2}$	$\frac{5}{3}$	$\frac{15}{8}$	2

Thus if we take middle C, as tuned to scientific pitch 256, the frequencies of the notes in its octave are

$$d^1: 256 \times \tfrac{9}{8} = 288,$$

$$e^1: 256 \times \tfrac{5}{4} = 320,$$

and so on.

It is very natural to inquire into the origin of this sequence of ratios. Notice that they are *simple* ratios, even though there is no apparent law governing their sequence.

The notes of the diatonic scale had become the basis of our music long before their frequencies were scientifically investigated. They were chosen because, to the European ear, they blended better than any others. They gave the maximum of concord.

We must therefore ask, why does one pair of notes give a pleasing concord and another pair an unpleasant discord? And why is it that concords are produced by notes whose frequencies bear a simple ratio to each other?

Discords are due to beats. When less frequent than about 10 per second beats can be distinguished separately, but when more frequent than this they give rise to a discord. The discord increases to a maximum of unpleasantness at a rate of beating of about 30 per sec., and does not disappear until a rate of about 80 per sec. (in the neighbourhood of middle C).

The unpleasant sensation is due to irritation of the ear, and may be compared to irritation of the eye caused by light flickering at a certain rate.

Now two notes which differ in frequency by more than 80 may still produce a discord; in this case the discord is due to beating between the overtones accompanying the fundamentals of these notes.

We have seen that strings and pipes whose lengths, and therefore frequencies, bear a simple ratio to each other have many overtones in common. It is therefore apparent why their notes when sounded together are likely to produce concord rather than discord.

Temperament.

Let us examine the intervals between the notes on the diatonic scale. We obtain these intervals by dividing the frequency of one note by that of its predecessor.

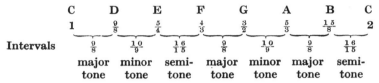

C	D	E	F	G	A	B	C
1	$\frac{9}{8}$	$\frac{5}{4}$	$\frac{4}{3}$	$\frac{3}{2}$	$\frac{5}{3}$	$\frac{15}{8}$	2

Intervals	$\frac{9}{8}$	$\frac{10}{9}$	$\frac{16}{15}$	$\frac{9}{8}$	$\frac{10}{9}$	$\frac{9}{8}$	$\frac{16}{15}$
	major tone	minor tone	semi-tone	major tone	minor tone	major tone	semi-tone

There are these three musical intervals which must be in the order shown.

The scale shown in Fig. 83 (*a*) is said to be the *key* of C, i.e. c is "doh", or the key-note. To give variety to a musical composition, or perhaps to bring a song within the compass of a singer, it is often desirable to be able to change the key, a process known as modulation.

Try playing a scale on the piano in the key of d, i.e. taking d as "doh". Two of the white keys will have to be replaced by black keys. The notes will be (see Fig. 83 (*b*)):

d^l	e^l	f^l♯	g^l	a^l	b^l	c^{ll}♯	d^{ll}
doh	ray	me	fah	soh	lah	te	doh^l

(f^l♯, called f sharp, is the note given corresponding to the black key between f^l and g^l and has a pitch intermediate between f^l and g^l: similarly c^{ll}♯ has a pitch intermediate between c^{ll} and d^{ll}.) Scales in other keys will require other black notes.

We have seen that (ignoring the distinction between major and minor tones and calling both tones), the order of the intervals in the diatonic scale must be—tone, tone, semitone, tone, tone, tone, semitone. But when we start with d and confine ourselves to the white keys of a piano the intervals are—tone, semitone, tone, tone, tone, semitone, tone. These intervals are in the wrong order. To make the second interval a full tone instead of a semitone we must use f♯ instead of f, and to make the last interval a semitone instead of a tone, we must use c♯ instead of c.

We can now see the use of the black notes on a piano. Unfortunately to make all the scales in the different possible keys correct, dozens of black notes would be necessary.

A compromise known as temperament is therefore necessary. Five black notes only—as many as fourteen have been tried in the past—are provided in each octave, giving the advantage of convenience in playing, but the disadvantage of slightly incorrect intervals in the different scales.

There are a number of methods of tempering but the scale of *equal temperament* is usually adopted, e.g. on the piano. We have seen that there are twelve notes and therefore twelve intervals in each octave on the piano keyboard. The octave intervals (2:1) alone are made correct and the twelve intervals in each octave are made exactly equal, i.e. $\sqrt[12]{2}:1$. It is surprising how nearly these intervals approximate to the intervals on the true diatonic scale.

	c	c♯	d	d♯	e	f	f♯
Ratios of frequencies on scale of equal temperament	1 1	$2^{\frac{1}{12}}$ 1·059	$2^{\frac{2}{12}}$ 1·122	$2^{\frac{3}{12}}$ 1·189	$2^{\frac{4}{12}}$ 1·260	$2^{\frac{5}{12}}$ 1·335	$2^{\frac{6}{12}}$ 1·414
Ratios of frequencies on true diatonic scale	1 1		$\frac{9}{8}$ 1·125		$\frac{5}{4}$ 1·250	$\frac{4}{3}$ 1·333	

	g	g♯	a	a♯	b	c
Ratios of frequencies on scale of equal temperament	$2^{\frac{7}{12}}$ 1·489	$2^{\frac{8}{12}}$ 1·587	$2^{\frac{9}{12}}$ 1·682	$2^{\frac{10}{12}}$ 1·782	$2^{\frac{11}{12}}$ 1·888	2 2
Ratios of frequencies on true diatonic scale	$\frac{3}{2}$ 1·500		$\frac{5}{3}$ 1·667		$\frac{15}{8}$ 1·875	2 2

The ratio of the frequencies of the notes of a piano on the scale of equal temperament and also on the true diatonic scale (in the key of C) are given above as fractions and decimals. Compare the values (in decimals) and see how closely they approximate.

In the case of the human voice and violin temperament is unnecessary. Why?

It is worth noting that we have been considering the major diatonic scale. There is also in use the minor diatonic scale with intervals, tone, semitone, tone, tone, tone, tone, semitone. The chromatic scale includes all the twelve white and black notes in the octave.

Measurement of loudness.

The loudness of a sound, like pitch, is a sensation in the mind. Just as the sensation of pitch is caused by the physical property of the waves—frequency—so the sensation of loudness is caused by what is termed the intensity of the waves. The intensity can be measured by the rate of flow of energy in the waves.

The loudness of a sound is not directly proportional to the intensity. The ear becomes less sensitive as intensity increases, according to the following law, discovered by Weber: "The extra stimulus required to produce a perceptible increase of sensation is proportional to the pre-existing stimulus."

Thus if the intensity of a sound is progressively doubled the loudness is not progressively doubled. It increases by equal additions.

Now if we keep multiplying a number by 2 this is equivalent to adding a constant logarithm to its logarithm. Hence the loudness of a sound is proportional to the logarithm of its intensity.

The unit of loudness most commonly used is the decibel, and loudness is expressed as so many decibels above the loudest sound an ear can just not detect, called the "threshold of audition".

$$\text{Number of decibels} = 10 \, \log_{10} \frac{E_1}{E_0},$$

where $E_1 =$ intensity of the given sound,
              $E_0 =$ intensity of the loudest sound an ear can just *not* detect.

If one sound is 100 times as intense as another sound, it is said to be 20 decibels louder: if it is 1000 times as intense, it is 30 decibels louder.

	Loudness decibels above threshold	Intensity energy flow watts per sq. cm.
Two circular saws at 3 ft.	110	13×10^{-6}
Loud motor horn at 100 ft.	100	1×10^{-7}
Ordinary conversation at 3 ft.	70	1×10^{-9}
Office with typewriters	60–50	$9 - 1 \times 10^{-11}$
Ticking of watch at 3 ft.	30	13×10^{-15}
Threshold of hearing	0	12×10^{-17}

Adapted from a paper on the "Measurement of Noise" by Churcher, King and Davis.

The above table shows the loudness and intensity of different sounds. The research on this question is of very recent date. The loudness and intensity of each noise was measured by comparing it with a note of frequency 800. Incidentally, the ear is much less sensitive to frequencies near the limits of audibility than to sounds of ordinary frequencies.

Another term, the *phon*, is also coming into use. If a sound has a loudness of 80 decibels above threshold, it is said to have a loudness of 80 phons.

The elimination of noise.

Considerable research is at present being conducted on the elimination of noise. Noise is here meant, not merely as sound

By courtesy of Messrs Metropolitan Vickers Electric Co. Ltd.

Fig. 84. An electric motor being tested for the noise it makes in a room lined with wool to prevent reverberation. Note the microphone which is picking up the sound.

of no recognisable pitch, but as unwanted sound, e.g. the hum of a motor or transformer or one's neighbour's wireless.

The troublesome noise in aircraft travel, tube railways and factories has been considerably reduced as a result of research. A recent report by the Departmental Committee of the Ministry of Transport has recommended that there should be a new "silence standard" of 90 phons, to which all mechanically propelled vehicles should conform.

SUMMARY

The action of the human ear is as follows. Sound waves enter the outer ear and set in vibration the ear drum. The vibrations of the ear drum are communicated via a compound lever consisting of three bones in the middle ear, to the oval window, the entrance to the inner ear, and thence via fluid to the basilar membrane in the cochlea, the organ of hearing. The basilar membrane consists of fibres connected by nerves to the brain and according to the resonance theory of hearing each fibre is set in vibration by a note of particular frequency, whereupon it sends a nerve current to the brain.

The musical interval between two notes of frequencies f_1 and f_2 is $\dfrac{f_2}{f_1}$: in the case of the octave this ratio is 2.

The frequencies of the notes of the **diatonic scale**, "doh, ray, me, fah, soh, lah, te, doh¹", are in the ratios $1:\frac{9}{8}:\frac{5}{4}:\frac{4}{3}:\frac{3}{2}:\frac{5}{3}:\frac{15}{8}:2$.

A piano has eight white and five black keys in each octave and the frequencies are in the ratio $1:2^{\frac{1}{12}}:2^{\frac{2}{12}}:2^{\frac{3}{12}}$, etc. This is known as the scale of equal temperament and makes possible scales with any note as the key-note (or "doh"), which closely approximate to the diatonic scale.

The loudness of a note is measured in decibels.

Number of decibels $= 10 \log_{10} \dfrac{E_1}{E_0}$ (see p. 119).

QUESTIONS

1. Describe the action of the human ear.
2. Write a brief account of the resonance theory of hearing.
3. Describe briefly the meaning of:
   - (a) A musical interval.
   - (b) The diatonic scale.
   - (c) Equal temperament.
4. Describe a simple form of siren and explain how it may be used to show that (a) the pitch of a note depends upon the frequency of

vibration, (b) the musical interval between two notes depends only on the ratio of their vibration frequencies. (L.)

5. Two musical sounds may differ from one another in three ways. Explain these differences, illustrating your answer with diagrams.

(L.)

6. Describe an experiment to show that the difference in pitch between two notes depends only on the ratio of the frequencies of the vibrating sources.

If you are given two notes whose vibration frequencies are 288 and 450, what is the vibration number of the note whose pitch is midway between them? (L.)

7. On what does the difference in pitch between two notes depend?

A note of frequency 384 is said to be a "fifth" higher in pitch than one of 256. What is the frequency of the note a "fifth" higher than the 384 note? What is the difference in pitch between it and the note?

(L.)

8. Describe the determination of the frequency of a tuning-fork by means of a siren. What assumption is made in the method of determining frequency?

If the frequency of the middle C on a piano is 260, what is the frequency of the next higher C and of the note midway between them? (L.)

9. Find the frequencies of the notes of the diatonic scale when the lowest (key) note has a frequency of 120 c.p.s.

10. What are the ratios of the lengths of the air columns of eight test-tubes, containing water, which give the notes of the diatonic scale when one blows across their open ends?

11. (a) The fundamental of an open organ pipe is middle C. What notes of the diatonic scale are its first three overtones?

(b) If the pipe is closed at one end what notes now are its fundamental and first three overtones?

12. The limits of audibility of the normal human ear are frequencies of 20 and 20,000 c.p.s. approximately. How many octaves does this represent?

13. Why do some notes when sounded together produce a concord and others a discord?

Three notes of frequencies 150, 160 and 240 c.p.s. are sounded successively in pairs. Which pairs will give discord and which concord? Explain fully.

14. How does the loudness of a note depend on its intensity? Describe and explain the decibel scale of loudness.

ANSWERS

CHAPTER II (page 32)

8. 840 ft., 1400 ft.   **9.** 6600 ft., $27\frac{1}{6}$ ft. per sec.

10. 1630 ft.   **14.** 330·9 metres per sec.   **15.** 4·72 sec.

17. 5230 metres per sec.   **18.** 1230 metres per sec.

CHAPTER IV (page 60)

4. 442 cm.   **5.** (*a*) 180 c.p.s., $6\frac{1}{6}$ ft. (*b*) 180 c.p.s., $26\frac{1}{6}$ ft.

7. 80.   **9.** 140 c.p.s., 360 revolutions per min.

10. 152·5 c.p.s.   **12.** 250 c.p.s., 230·8 c.p.s.

13. 249·6 c.p.s., 230·4 c.p.s.   **14.** 112·7 c.p.s.

CHAPTER V (page 73)

4. 0·96 : 1.   **15.** (*a*) 280·4 c.p.s. (*b*) 38·34 cm.

16. $22\frac{2}{5}$ lb.   **17.** Increased 1·56 times.

CHAPTER VI (page 95)

3. 336 metres per sec.   **4.** 364·5 metres per sec.

5. 9·7 in.   **6.** 337·92 metres per sec.

19. 5×10^5 cm. per sec.   **20.** 930 ft. per sec.

CHAPTER VIII (page 121)

6. 360 c.p.s.   **7.** 576 c.p.s., 1·5.   **12.** 10.

INDEX